IMMORTALITY NOW AND FOREVER ~

HOW TO LIVE FOREVER IN YOUR DIVINE BODY OF LIGHT!

REVEREND DR. LIND

IMMORTALITY NOW & FOREVER!

How to Live Forever in Your Divine Body of Light!

PUBLISHED BY REVEREND DR. LINDA DE COFF
And
NEW THOUGHT INTERNATIONAL, INC.

Copyright at 2016 ~ Library of Congress

~

The ***Reverend Dr. Linda De Coff*** is the noted founder of **New Thought International, Inc.** (An Association of Global Centers for World Peace & Enlightenment). She is also the celebrated author of the stunning evolutionary series of books ~ Global Divine Consciousness, on the next step in spiritual advancement for the greatest benefit of all Humanity.

Dr. Linda has spoken nationally and internationally on Highest Consciousness Themes, and was honored to receive her Doctorate at the United Nations 50th Anniversary. Dr. Linda combines the best of the East and the West in her timeless teachings of Truth.

IMMORTALITY NOW & FOREVER

INTRODUCTION

"LIFE AT THE SUMMIT (Life From the Summit Point of View)!"

~ REVEREND DR. LINDA DE COFF

Dear Reader:

In this book on the Immortal Essence of our ever on-going lives, Dr. Linda poses the provocative question: Are death, dying disease and aging ideas born of Spiritual Perfection, or are they of the Mortal Mind…an imposition on the vital life of God, animating every cell and atom of each and every being that exists?

If not, perhaps *"Now is the Time"* to let go of these debilitating concepts forever, and begin to live our every moment from the consciousness of our Divine and Immortal Life and Gifts, running through our very bloodstream, learning how to avail of the radiant properties, and enhance every moment by living in the consciousness of utmost Realities…abiding forever in the elixir of Divine Truth, bringing Heaven to Earth!

Dr. Linda reveals the luminous Truths of Being and offers Enlightening Keys on How to Extend Your Life indefinitely, through the realization of the "Immortal I Am within." ~ ever transcendent of time and experience, ever empowered to rise anew.

In the realization of your Immortality Now and Forever, you will never be the same and all of life will resonate in new-found freedom, love, light and joy.

Let us know ourselves as God knows us to be. Let us rise victorious and bless our every waking moment with the Divine Breath taking us far and beyond issues of the past. Through the consciousness of our Immortality Now and Forever, death, disease and dying can become a thing of the past, as the Immortal, ever-renewing components of Divine life itself cause us to extend our lives on this plane or any other, just as far as we choose Let our lives pulsate with the radiance of the Sublime. Rejoice as you meet your Divine and Eternal Self!

So Be It ~ And So It Is!

"THE ULTIMATE PROMISE"

"I am Ageless ~ Birthless ~ Deathless Being."

EXCERPT ~ SONGS OF ETERNITY

Beloved:

The purest Truth of body is that it is the most exquisite temple and manifestation of the perfection of God ~ the microcosm in the great macrocosm ~ as orderly as the planets in their orbits ~ as luminous as the stars ~ as harmonious in function, as the most awesome symphony. The fulfillment of the ultimate promise and conversion into the Golden Body of Light ~ is the blessing for all, who realize this.

The fact is we are the *Eternal Resurrection*; and upon truest illumination; complete transformation and transfiguration, indeed, take place. When you spend time making sure that only constructive thoughts pour through every atom of your life system, the Light within begins to release and pour out, even through the skin ~ reflecting the luminous content of your golden mind and heart.

As Emerson said: "Every thought is scripted on our face." A person's mental and emotional content cannot be hid. Let your body reflect the *God-Light* of your being. Let all body systems report the Truth of your great harmony and an infinite perfection residing in you, now.

Know and ever affirm: "I am the Resurrection and the Life" ~ eternally transmitting my *God Essence* through myself ~ mentally, emotionally, physically in all my ways. My nervous system is the great harmonic symphony of God."

And So It Is!

Now, let us delve into the supreme healing powers of the Divine Self within, unfolding the transcendent strengths, powers and capacities of the One True Self. Know that each time you center in Highest Consciousness, you are now poised to experience instant miracles, as the reservoir of perfect and unlimited healing energy is freed within you. So, keep your most cherished goals of transcendent freedom uppermost in your mind, as we journey together to explore the Immortal Life and stellar attributes that are already ours.

For those who wish to truly incorporate Immortal and self-existent aspects of the eternal Life Principles ~ throughout this book, enjoy the profound consciousness raising exercises and soaring meditations… for your very practical application and utmost elevation of your soul.

Be sure and take plenty of time, as you read through the empowering chapters, contemplating each for as long as you need to incorporate the consciousness-raising summit ideas being considered, applying to your every moment and towards the actualization of you every noble goal.

Always strive to live above and beyond any experiences of the moment, realizing that "There is nothing that cannot be healed, perfected and transformed through the perfect Immortal Life and pure Light of God within you."

CONTENTS

MEDITATIONS FOR CENTERING IN THE IMMORTAL TRUTH

OTHER HELPFUL LINKS

IMMORTALITY NOW AND FOREVER ~

HOW TO LIVE FOREVER IN YOUR DIVINE BODY OF LIGHT!

CHAPTER ONE

LIVING YOUR IMMORTALILTY NOW!

Living Your Immortality Now!

"THE ULTIMATE PROMISE"

I AM THAT I AM!

AND RIGHT NOW I DECLARE
THESE WORDS...THROUGHOUT ALL OF CONSCIOUSNESS ~
SO THAT EVERY SENSE, CELL AND VITAL FACULTY OF
FORM AND FUNCTION MAY HEAR AND RESPOND TO THE
GLORIOUS TRUTH!

I AM ONE WITH THAT WHICH IS SUBLIME AND ETERNAL...
A PERFECT, BEAUTIFUL BODY PATTERN OF PURE GOD-
LIGHT!

I AM ONE WITH GOD IN ALL!
MY SOUL'S PATTERNS AND MEMORIES NOW RESPOND
TO THE EXQUISITE TRUTH OF EXISTENCE ~
I AM AGELESS, DEATHLESS, BIRTH LESS BEING.

NO MATTER WHAT ENCUMBRANCES
I HAVE ACCEPTED OR ACCUMULATED AROUND ME ~
I NOW STAND FREE TO LIVE AND BEAR WITNESS TO THIS
DIVINE FACT ~
ESTABLISHED FROM THE BEGINNING!

MY BODY CAN NO LONGER BECOME OR BE A WASTE-BIN
FOR NEGATIVE SPECULATION, PROJECTION OR
ACTIVITIES...NO MORE!
I BELIEVE IN AND UPHOLD, LIVE AND REFLECT ~
THE DIVINE PATTERN AT ALL TIMES!

I AM A BODY OF LIGHT...KNOWING!

Reverend Dr. Linda De Coff

NO MATTER WHAT I REMEMBER NOW WHO I AM
AND MY RESURRECTED BODY TELLS THE
WELCOME TRUTH ~
AS EVERY MOLECULE OF DIVINE INTELLIGENCE
ACCELERATES, RAISES AND VIBRATES
WITH UNFATHOMABLE BRILLIANT LIGHT!

I KEEP MY CONSCIOUSNESS ON HIGH
AND LET CHRIST LIGHT
RESTORE MY EVERY ATOM, TISSUE AND FIBER OF BEING!

THANK YOU GOD! I AM THE RESURRECTION
AND THE LIFE ~
THE WHOLE DIVINE IDEA MADE MANIFEST…
ON EVERY LEVEL AND IN EVERY WAY!

I REJOICE ~ I AM THE KINGDOM OF HEAVEN
COME TO EARTH
AND ESTABLISHED IN MY BODY-BEING
AND RECORDED IN MY SOUL'S BLUEPRINT!

I AM ETERNAL LIFE LIVING FOREVER IN A BODY OF
LIGHT!

~ AND SO IT IS!

MEDITATION EXCERPT FROM "SONGS OF ETERNITY ~
CONTEMPLATIONS, TREATMENTS & MEDITATIONS
ON THE WORD OF GOD!"

CHAPTER ONE

LIVING YOUR IMMORTALITY NOW!

As we begin our ascent in consciousness to grasp the lustrous Immortal Truth of Being, I encourage the reader to take a moment to just relax and let go all thought-taking, and right now take a deep breath to the count of seven if you can, and then hold seven, and then release once again to the count of seven, twenty-one being the Divine number of completion. If you are unable, do what you can. This is centering and preparing to receive of illumination from the Divine center of yourself.

Now then, in order to access our Highest Good, we must know that this Highest Good (the ultimate potential expression for every aspect of life) is already resident in our Highest Consciousness, the summit, where we may sit in the regal place at the right hand of the Father. The point of breathing so deeply, richly and fully, filling every cell and atom of being with the Light of God, is not only to regenerate every atom of being, but to bring that consummate Divine energy up ~ to bring the breath up ~ to circulate

1

the Divine Breath, not only increasing and rejuvenating brain cells, but bringing the energy up to make contact with the Ultimate and Highest point of Consciousness within.

Herein forever exists the complete substance of all your good. When we say the Kingdom of Heaven, we mean the Kingdom of Heaven is the Kingdom of Highest Consciousness ~ Highest Awareness of ourselves as one with the Infinite, one with the primal Light that animates and empowers all of being.

So to us, our good is the completeness of Divine Life ~ and I love this equation of what the Divine Name of God means – we know that the all-inclusive name of "God" equals every form of good. So whatever the good is that you have in mind for yourself, know that this objective is God- in- you right now, the substance of richest Divine Life in expression that you are seeking to bring forth. That is how the substance of God appears to you…in a form that you can personally recognize and that speaks to you of the Divine Presence and Power…that speaks to you of fulfillment.

In the wonderful book, "When You Can Walk On Water, Take the Boat" ~ the author recounts his very moving story of how he met God in his life, in a most personal and meaningful way. He had suffered much difficulty in his business and finances, and was seeking a new position. Through a series of miraculous encounters rich in Divine Guidance, the protagonist was led to seek a position in

2

a top-notch firm. In one instance, he walks into the office of a very large and successful company located on the top floor of a soaring building that stretched high into the skies. He had obtained an appointment with the President, God. God's offices were all in white with the most glorious architecture, and when he entered he was greeted with aplomb and welcomed by the President, God itself, appearing as a very well-appointed man in a marvelous white suit, who then proceeded to choose him for the highly desirable position.

Here was God, speaking to him in a way he could recognize, becoming the completeness of the healing good sought. This is how the Law of Mind and manifestation works for us, when we are centered in Divine and fulfilling ideas, whether it be a business position, a perfect relationship, perfect healing from some traumatic event.

So remember this. When you are thinking in terms of good for yourself, whatever that might be, whether it is defense, whether it is protection, whether it is supply, whether it is support ~ always know, as the great Emma Curtis Hopkins says, "God is my support. God is my supply. God is my unfailing answer to every prayer and to the healing of every condition imaginable." When we call upon the Divine Name for whatever we need, this Divine Substance turns into utmost solution, through the stream of our conscious knowing, recognition and acceptance, moving upon the waters of being to become, on the physical manifest level, that which

3

we so desire. So it really behooves us to commune in that place from whence all our good does come ~ the place on High, Divine Mind, in us ~ not afar off, but right within the depths of our very own soul, the flame of Divine Life always moving to become the likeness of our thought.

Through meditation and Spiritual Mind Treatment, we contact the Divine Source within. Treatment is the most elevated form of prayer, wherein we recognize the completeness and power of the Divine Presence and Power regarding our situations, rising far transcendent of circumstances into the Divine Realm, where all answers exist. And for those of you who aren't familiar, know that when we become conscious beings, aware of the power of ourselves, we also move into the domain where we understand we are responsible for the flow of our thoughts, realizing our experience depends upon what we are thinking into the Creative Mind.

Throughout the metaphysical world, Treatment is regarded as the most powerful tool, the consummate way of using your mind definitely in perfect order to establish a new current in your thinking pattern that forms a mold that then allows the experience sought to come through. Treatment is so very powerful because it aligns you with your Divine Source, the very Truth of your being, over, above and beyond, and regardless of your experience, and powers you in a clear, focused direction, where the all-encompassing mind of God can respond in full to you.

The lustrous subject of our thought throughout this book is about "Living your Immortality Now" and the implications of arriving at that state of consciousness that transforms all in your world, and brings you very definitely and immediately to Higher States of Being and experience than ever before. Let us prepare.

SETTING THE GOAL

Now, breathing in and out of the radiance and completeness of Divine Life ~ Think of yourself in the purity of Highest Light, in your original body of perfection, before destructive habits formed ~ in the radiance of pure Divine Light. Every aspect of yourself, your atomic body is pulsating with the Light of Perfection.

Ask yourself, where have I gone off course? Is this natural to the Divine Me? If not, be willing to shed it all that you may return in all of body, mind and being to the beneficence of First Cause.

Now, taking a deep breath of peace and newly absorbing the perfection of the one Divine Self, return to the present, and remember all that you now want to change, all destructive habits you want to let go of for the sake of the Divine You; all that you want to transform and uplift, merging in the pure life of the most High ~ that you may extend your life indefinitely, recognizing always only one First Cause, One Presence and Power of unconditional Love and Light, reigning supreme over all in your world.

5

It is something else, a new and Divine world… to live from that consciousness that you are, as all the great masters have said, the Infinite, Eternal, Light and Energy of God-in-action, moving throughout your experiences, throughout lifetimes. With a consciousness and an awareness of your Immortal and Eternal existence filling your every moment, it stirs up that fabulousness, that profound and unassailable courageousness, knowing every step you take shall be victorious, catapulting you to a very Divine state of being, unleashing that Light of Faith that lets you know that regardless of whatever is in front of you now, that obstruction shall pass. You shall overcome, because of the life of God in you.

We are assured that as soon as we have discovered the Divine Principle inherent in any challenging experience and fully activated in our life and situation, that experience will release us, will dissolve to forever flow downstream into the nothingness from which it arose, and we are then eternally free to go on. It is so wonderful to know that nothing has come to devastate us. Everything has come to empower us, and when we do become clear about a thing and ascend into our Divine relationship with it, we also simultaneously become free of the need for it to ever occur again. And that is part of the real Eternality of our Spirit ~ that problems were never the goal. The goal of life is not to throw you ceaseless problems, nor for you to go round and round the karmic wheel over and over again, never rising out. The goal of life is your forever emancipation.

That is what that lustrous Spirit within you wants you to achieve, through coming clear about whatever your situations are now, introducing the Divine Principle that brings you above and forever victorious, never to descend again.

It is very exciting for me that we are now beginning to look deeply at the Truth of our Immortal Being, which is where we derive our power and ability to transcend, and that we can charge up and continue our ongoing ascension into the more powerful, more masterful life that is ours by Divine Right. The greatest you can think of is the Kingdom and is yours by Divine Right. Not only is it yours by Divine Right, it is the right of every being and everything that lives and moves and has life. Fullest expression of the Immortal life that you are, in the now, ever and anon is the sublime right of every being. There is no horizon too great to attain and nothing that cannot be achieved in the ever-increasing Light.

The destiny of each and all is to come fully over and above the karmic wheel of repetition. Every time a challenge is confronted, we want to move to a greater place with it, achieving levels of even greater victory and overcoming, a radiant expansion of success never before experienced.

Thus, we are looking at the most important subject of *Immortality* and discovering how, through the total embodiment and incorporation in every fiber of our being of this fundamental Truth

7

of our nature, we may rise free of every single negative force that has held us in its grip for eons or however long you think you've been going through a particular experience.

It is only through the cognition of your Immortality that you can reach deep into your etheric body to release those things that bind you, and it has a very far-reaching affect, far beyond the fact that you'll live longer and your life will be a better expression.

The realization of your Immortality in the now and not sometime later flows out to affect, touch and bless every aspect of your life. Realize your supply, your relationships, your entire attitude on life is governed by what you think of your life. So if you think of it as having a beginning and an end and that is it, then you are missing the whole point. Yet, if you think of every step being a Divine opportunity to rise ever higher, you will gain all the maximum benefit that such a glorious attitude can bring.

Every relationship then, and every effort now becomes an opportunity to express and cultivate the greater in you.

Jesus, the "Christ" said, "I have come that ye may have life and have it more abundantly." What that means, also, is that you shall know the glorious truth of your true freedom and your being, and this quintessential knowing shall make you free. Because once you know the Truth, you can no longer take the position of victim.

Now, you know you are one with that incomprehensible power that is you ~ that is your life.

"I, the Truth, have come to wake you up that you may have more life and have it more abundantly." Ernest Holmes, Jesus, the Buddha, every great consciousness that every blessed us has always said, "You are as Immortal now as you ever shall be."

In other words, Immortality is not something that is down the line, taking place after you die and go to Heaven. Heaven is a state of mind, and thus Immortality is not something we attain. It is something that we have. It is something that we are.

And this is so important to realize – that everything and every result in life rests on what you are identified with, the purest Truth or something less.

Ask, "What am I deeply identifying myself with?" "Am I identifying myself with mortality, limitation, helplessness, hopelessness? Or am I identifying myself with the Source of my being and all that that Divine and all-encompassing Source is about?" Obviously, that has to include Immortality.

"Before Abraham was, I am." "I knew you before you were in the womb." Life is a journey of Infinite Spirit throughout the many mansions.

When we look outside ourselves, we notice that life seems to have a way of going on. Things change, there are transformations, leaves drop to the ground and trees seem to be bare and lifeless in the silence of winter, but everything rises up anew, ever growing and regenerating from within, everything continues on an Infinite and Eternal Cycle ~ and that is us, the fundamental Truth of our nature, for we are one with all that that is.

Realize, all Divine Power and Capacity along with all the radiant qualities of Infinite Life are within us all. Thus, we are indeed as Immortal now as we ever shall be.

There is the timeless statement that the spiritual man/woman is already perfect, and this is such a powerful statement to realize in terms of curing our cases of mistaken identity. When identified with the great Truth of our limitless being within, then we know truly there is nothing to "fix". There is only the Great Truth to realize and bring out, applying its healing balm to every aspiration, as you release the *Divine You*. Thus, always know that regardless of whatever may seem to be going on, you are also, right now, in your Spiritual Reality, just as perfect and complete and whole as ever you shall be, and you shall find the perfect way of transcending, because of God-in-you.

Now whether or not we are expressing this ultimate Truth in "all our ways" is the only question we ever need to ask, and is where we are working throughout this book.

But regardless of whatever level you are expressing, the Truth of your Being always is. Since you are manifest of Divine Substance, you are what it is, and you shall always be that.

To the degree that we are aware of it, we attain happiness. To the degree that we feel separate from it, we are unhappy, and we are living in limitation and shortage because we are cut off from the main source of our being

.

Does anyone feel that we actually created ourselves? I don't think so. We gain of our limitless creative powers from the Most High. There is that radiant something, which we call God, Divine Mind, the Great Source of the many Divine Names, that breathed life into all that is, as an expression of itself, a manifestation of Eternal and Immortal life. Einstein says energy goes nowhere, and so it is the same thing for the Divine Human, for energy cannot be diminished; only transformed. Thus, our own lives may transform into Divine Life…to the degree one's consciousness has embraced the Infinite and Eternal Truth.

How can the awesomely great beings that have blessed humanity throughout the ages, and even our own life become so great, as we really come into living from the consciousness of our Immortality, advancing one stellar step forward in our evolution?

How can the saints and sages and avatars throughout time lay claim to this blockbusting fact? Truly it is a blockbusting, eternal fact that we are Immortal simply for the reason that humankind is a manifestation of God, born of the mind of God, an idea of God, the life of God made manifest, as beloved Jesus, the greatest metaphysical teacher that ever was ~ let us know. "The Father is within." "I am in the Father, and the Father is in me."

The Supreme Architect manifested itself just for its good pleasure as us… unique representations of all that Infinite Spirit is.

We also realize, simultaneously ~ and it just makes good sense ~ that the Original Cause can only manifest that which it is. Would any architect or innovator desire to remove their own impress from their creation? No. So too, we indeed must bear the signs of the Original Cause, the Divine causation to all that is. Thus the pure pattern and Infinite potential of ourselves ever exists in the Mind of God, compelling from deep within.

The Higher Mind of each and all is commensurate with the Divine nature, with all that is complete, whole, and perfect ~ the total expression of pure life, Divine Order, symmetry, balance, perfection, unity, beauty, strength, power. Infinite potential for all forms of expression and Eternal Hope now rises before us ~ in the profound realization that there are endless horizons of mental, physical, emotional and spiritual well-being that may be attained.

Jesus said, "Our God is a God of the living." The Jewish race proclaimed, "Behold, Our God is one God." "One God." From every angle, you get the message, and God, we know, equals the eternal risen prototype of ourselves, of our every form of good. "Our God is a God of the living." That means God is the energy of life, the resurrected one. Envision yourself as Immortal Life, continuously rising to greater and greater levels of Divine Light, Love, and all that is God. When we come in touch with the wholeness and capacity of our Divine Self, we then get a new idea, a greater idea of ourselves, and at that moment of realization, we are empowered with new energy to resurrect and to overcome.

With a consciousness of the Immortality of Being, life rises to embrace Eternity in the now, taking on a new context entirely, and a new hope of reaching Higher and Higher levels and states of every level of existence, including attaining highest stages of physical well-being.

Haven't we resurrected a million times? You go in and out of experiences, and with enough added consciousness, you always overcome. Well, what do you think the Resurrection is? Know our God is the very essence of eternally renewing life, a God of the living, of resurrection in and through every good thing for the awakened. Live from the consciousness of your Immortality Now and you will never have reason to quit or give up, yet hope shall adorn you with wings of ascent that know no horizon or limit.

13

The sublime destiny of all of us is to become completely conscious of that glory of the Divine nature which we are and to be able to utilize that very practically in our everyday worlds. Thus we see now that any temporary problems, illnesses, lacks, challenges, deaths, difficulties, defeats which manifest through our body or through our physical world, which we also call "body" ~ (anything we can touch, feel, see out there is called the body... the "body of circumstances", "physical body", "body of relationships"), all exterior is the reflection of the inner state of consciousness, and can be corrected by consciousness. Our problems, all of the lacks, death itself, denial ~ all difficulties appearing on the outer emanate from the root misconception that "I am mortal", and therefore limited. How far can consciousness go, when restricted by such thinking?

Can you hear what I'm saying? In the complete life of God, there can be no death. That is why Jesus said, "My Father is a God of the living." There is no concept of death. If there were any truth to mortality, everything that is related to breakdown or lack or limitation would rend the fabric of the universe. If there were any principle of lack, and if there weren't a self-existent Principle of Abundance, the universe would have broken down. If there literally were a principle in the fabric of life called death, as a self-existent force, worlds would die and the energy would not transmute and be reborn. So we need to stop planning to die, and we need to live with the lustrous consciousness, "I'm always birthing," in the sense that I am always moving into greater awareness ~ into greater expression

14

of myself. Feel the momentum of your Divine Soul, ever rising higher to embrace every mansion of Divine and Glorious Life.

Learn to stop putting these time limits on your Divine and Immortal Self, i.e., "I've got so many years to live. That's it. Oh, I guess my time is up, and I should decay this body now." Well what for? If life is always regenerating itself, what do you have to do that for? Don't you know your molecules are moving every moment, and taking shape moment to moment according to your consciousness?

If your mind is on Light and the Love of the Creator all the time, isn't your physical instrument going to express that which you are thinking? Won't the beneficence of your thought flow through every atom and cell of your being? And so it is with everything and every aspect of your life. The Truth that all is a manifestation of consciousness is so helpful to know and it is such a blessing when you come to the lustrous point in your evolution where you know that you know beyond a shadow of a doubt that there is no truth to, "I have to die. I have to lack. I have to take it. I've got to experience limitation."

Regardless of whatever you are going through at the moment, know that somehow the greatness within you will bring you through it, and you shall discover the Truth. At that very point of discovering the Truth of your Immortal being, ever one with the Most High, you shall become free, and you shall see a greater manifestation.

15

To me, that is endless wonder to behold and endless in import. It means I never have to stop in my evolution, in the sense of getting freer and more joyous, as I live and cultivate my soul's path of eternal evolution. All negative speculation about ourselves is a mere case of mistaken identity… that we are mortal. We are Spirit and we are Law. You know the saying, "I'm only human. It's my fate." How great it is to know, there is no such a thing, and no Truth to the notion that we are separate from God and doomed from the start.

How many have felt doomed at some point in their life ~ doomed to go around some type of endless repetition? Well that is not the Divine Story. No true God of boundless life could dream of that fruitless destiny for you. God does not dream of your destruction and doom. God dreams of your emancipation. It is only the human that has misconstrued Divine Purpose and intent.

How could that Sublime One, the breath of our life, which is breathing in and through us right now and which we are utilizing every moment right now, which has expressed itself as us, radiant ideas of itself and what it is ~ how could we inherently express anything other than what we are ~ the Immortal Life of Spirit ever unfolding and creating? Do we really have to continue our deep pact with death, or shall we rise to embrace a new identity and greater concept of ourselves as one with the very atom and essence of complete life, knowing no death, no lack nor defeat?

What happens when we transcend the idea that death, which equals the greatest idea of giving-upness and failure that ever was invented, the greatest burden to the Divine Life and aspiration of the human ~ what happens when we relate and think and live according to the secret silent truth of our Immortality? What happens?

Is there any Truth to time? Isn't time just a human construct, to help us live in a structured orderly sense? Yet, there is no force called time pressing upon us, causing aging, dying and decay. Once I was blessed to have 3 generations of students, unfolding in glory before me, mother, daughter and grandmother. As they continued in their avid studies of Truth, the gap in so-called "years" simply disappeared, with all three sporting the gorgeousness of the Light of the Infinite and Divine Soul...the lustrous, timeless Light Body within emerging forth.

Realize, when you take on something new, a greater idea...something must go. When you put on the new "wineskin" of elevated thought, when you take on the new consciousness of yourself, indeed you leave behind that domain of death, fear and separation from the Source of your Life, which is just a lot of hearsay passed down through centuries, acting as a veil of separation. Basking now in the sun of Divine Illumination, the individual soul leaves the dual dimension, where he or she was living defensively, caught up in trying to survive, believing there was inevitable death ~ now entering the beatitude of Life Eternal.

17

Realize that every ounce of anxiety is rooted in trying to survive as a physical body. When you can release that and realize the Truth of your Immortal Spirit, that deep, deep anxiety will just stream away from the depths of your consciousness. You will stop living defensively because you are no longer caught up in trying to survive against an inevitability, and you will move up in consciousness to realize, "I am the life of God, and my body is a perfect idea of God made manifest." What else could it be? For there is not a spot where God is not.

In the Light of Lustrous Truth, life is emancipated in the Divine human. All that one has been compelled to do under the belief that life is short, all the desperate living now converts and conforms to be an energy of ever increasing Faith and Light. That energy that was so bound up in defensive living is now free to go out to transform and to rise, to radiate eternally the greater concept that you now know, regardless of your circumstances, about yourself: "I am that I am always", "My God-Light body is always," and "every aspect of my life is always the every self-renewing action of spirit."

Now here is another great concept to consider deeply.

Once you release the notion of inevitable death, ask what can there be? Herein, you will discover the great Principle of Renewal. If there is no stopping, and there is only continual life, then there is a Principle of Self-Renewal.

18

Now you will think of yourself in a new way… "I am the ever-self-renewing action of spirit in my life, in my body, in my careers, in my relationships ~ rising ever into greater dimensions of unfoldment, as I embrace the Greater Reality within my soul." "I am that which shall always rise again. Whatever it is I'm dealing with, I am that which shall always rise again." With this risen consciousness, do we need to maintain any futility or despair about that which we are and our inevitable victory over any matter? Thus, if something doesn't seem to go right in the moment, just know that: "I am that which shall always rise again."

Once, at the end of a phase in my life ~ where I was changing careers, and in transition from the acting scene (which I loved), yet did not know what was greater or what was next…I had a dream where I was dressed in black and where I was walking down a road, with my back facing my view and my face veiled in the front.

As I witnessed this dream, I wondered what could be the message, and suddenly a voice said, very powerfully and from the depths of my being ~ "I shall come again!"

And so it was, that soon after this prophecy of the future, the new step came forward and I switched to metaphysics and study of Truth and ultimately to ministry, for even greater than all the wonderful leading roles and optimum experiences I had had as a performer, there was more for me. God was just moving me into the realm of Greater Truth, far more encompassing, far more rewarding than any career of the past, than anything else I had ever done.

Can we live in the question, in the times of change, knowing there is always Greater to come, yet another envelope of Divine Destiny to open wide, to arise from the endless fountain of guidance within? The most powerful statement/mantra you can say over any circumstances is: "I am the Resurrection and the Life."

That affirmation of itself will open the whole matter up, unseal the secret doors of Divine Solution, and reveal the perfect pathway of rising above. Know ~ "I shall always rise again".

When these sacred words of the glory of the Divine Self came to me as I was contemplating this book, when I realized the profundity of this mantra and all that it means for every human being, I was bowled over, and thrilled beyond measure. How fantastic that this empowering Principle resides in each and every one of us! So that means there is nothing that I or you won't overcome, and no horizon too great to aspire to. Rather, I and you shall move towards the Truth eternally, closer and closer to the Truth of our being, always and ever. Isn't that great?

If I am that which doesn't know death, then I must have built in my living faculties the ability to have self-renewing power. How many times have we changed our physical shape at will? Whatever

20

one's desire may be, a desire to be lighter, heavier, whatever it may be, we simply change the course of destiny by getting a new concept, seeing ourselves there, and the outer automatically begins to conform to the new idea. How free we really all are.

With the word of Truth, the body then conforms to the new and lustrous pattern we have set for it. If we are in right action - if we are acting accordingly with our words, by speaking, knowing and claiming the Truth of our Immortal Selves, we are guaranteed outstanding success.

Once again, ask why do I have this self-renewing power built in me, already present? Who is the giver of this great Gift of Life? All of us have this Master Power, for that which made us is complete, perfect and whole, and it could not have made you or me missing any parts or abilities. In this Truth , we gain a dynamic new sense of courage, a new buoyancy and sense of ourselves as free. And we can afford now, knowing who we are, to live and love again. For we are that which never runs out of the ability for love no matter what "they", any person, place or circumstance has done to us. We are one with all the love that is ~ ever self-renewing.

Just because we are love, we can be love, not just because someone was nice to us on a particular day, but because that is the Divine and Immortal essence of who we are. Just because we are the Immortal, *Self-Renewing* Light of God in our every cell and etheric

21

structure, we can rise to be that health of being that overcomes a world of infirmities.

So I can afford to live and love knowing who I am and with a total sense of the inevitability of all forms of good, with knowledge of my Divine Rights to express the Highest and the Best, with all consciousness of complete life and potential being mine, knowing that Life Itself has all interest in my triumph.

Immortality now means that if there is hurt, trauma, the whatever(s) that come in life, the challenges that come in life ~ it doesn't matter how great the challenges appear, what they are or what they look like, they all constitute the same thing to us now, some thought of separation from the Divine Life that we are. With this knowledge ~ each can rise free and always know the Greater Truth: "I am ever self-renewing, and I have the power to rise above every emotional trauma through the greatness of this Divine and Immortal Love that I am." "I shall rise again." It means lifetimes may come and go; yet "I shall rise again, for there is no end to me."

Ideas of beginnings and endings now dissolve from our consciousness.

There is no beginning, and there is no end. There is only an ever on-goingness of Spirit and that which always is. And that is us, the Purity of the Divine Soul ever unfolding, ever becoming more.

Rather now, we rise up to see a complete movement of an ever-complete life, moment to moment taking a certain mold or form. Think of how life really is. For instance, you have one career, and then you get new ideas, and pretty soon you are manifesting another career, right? By the content and projection of our thought, energy takes a form, appropriate for a while, then we release it, and that same Divine and Infinite Substance flows free to take another form according to our liking, and this is the eternal movement of that complete energy of life. Thus it is that our inner ideas form a mold for a certain form of manifestation, and just as easily, we can release that energy, and put it into a new form. But the substance itself is always ours. It never leaves us, Divine clay in our hands to change the structures of our world in an instant.

Change is a hallmark of the creative power in us. This Divine Creative spark within us does not want to be fixed forever in a certain dimension or form, thinking that "this is the totality of me." How could Infinite Spirit ever want to be stuck in a certain equation? That is impossible for the unbound. Just know that we shall always be shifting and changing and expanding eternally. There is no stop to that ever ongoing urge towards greater expression, for we are the creative life of limitless God-in-action. That is who we are.

Now, in this lofty realization, we let go of expecting endings. We do perform closure on things. We do leave things behind, but it is always now with more of a sense of flowingness and

23

continuity. "If that job, that relationship is complete and done, and served its purpose in my life, now I'm moving on to this next thing." And we identify now with the ever-moving action of ever-new spirit. Life and lifetimes then become, for us, as the great Emerson said, some parts of the greater flow of life and the great expression. Some part of that great, great, great whole. So now doomsday is out. It just doesn't work in the Divine System. It does not exist in the Divine System, and so too, it should not exist for us.

We "become like Him", like the cause of all existence ~ in our countenance, our greater thoughts immediately reflective throughout our physical form. This is why you always see the Buddha laughing. Christ said, "Be joyous." He came for you to let go of suffering and to show the model of how to rise free and live in perpetual joy. The whole being now transforms, as we become more and more like him in all our ways. Our very physical bodies start to have a different molecular arrangement because the thoughts that are flowing through them are more harmonious and lighter. There is even a molecular change that goes on with this correction in our thinking, and continuous evolution of the Divine element in our very DNA strands and in every gene.

And we begin to literally radiate Divine Light from every cell of our being. Some people call this the aura. Some people call it your atmosphere. Your atmosphere is that invisible radiation of the sum total of what you are thinking and feeling.

As you begin to radiate this new, great knowing about the Light of your Being, you are now fulfilling that promise. Renew your spirit in the elixir of Divine Truth. We have renewed our spirit because we now know who we are. Some part of us deep within knows we are one with God, and that is it. Period. This cannot be rationalized. It is a given. There is no argument that can stand against that which is True. Each is one with God...One with the Supreme Radiance. That something eternal exists now, grounded firm in our reality, a mighty force beyond all other ideas.

Have you ever felt yourself in the lowest emotional state?" I feel down, I feel stuck, I feel whatever", yet somehow knowing, "This is not right. There must be a way out. There must be a way out." Even in such moments of deepest, darkest despair, isn't there something about the human spirit that feels there must be a way out and seeks it? That is that Fire of Truth within us, compelling us not to accept the limitation. Why should anyone be doomed to ultimate failure and separation? Who said this about me? About you? Who said it? Not God. Not the source of your being.

Now let us look even further into the beneficent import of living in the awareness of your Immortal life in God. Here are some of the implications. Let me just clarify this for you again. You are Immortal. That means there is no time that you have to die. With the right maintenance, you may keep your body flowing in grace, ever maintain consciousness and perfection of form, ever self-renewing, as long as you want. There is no failure. There is only an ever-increasing understanding of who and what you are, causing every effort, saturated in the healing balm of greater realization, to pour forth greater and greater fruit. "There is only success." You are that which is one with successful being. God did not fail in manifesting this planet. You shall not fail in manifesting what you desire ~ your every good and noble desire, as your mind is stayed on your Immortal essence, one with the Light, one with Father/Mother God.

There is no failure. There is no lack. There is no limitation. All these notions are of the death module. These ideas alone are the very force that takes us down. You are ever self-renewing. You have that promise. "I am ever self-renewing. I am a Master of my Destiny in the Light. I self-renew. I self-renew in and through every experience."

Some of the other radiant implications that dawn upon consciousness, when we take on and consciously own and don the cloak of our Divine Immortality, are that we also realize the substance of life cannot diminish or run out. And, this knowing alone governs all manifestations of Supply. It wouldn't make sense. If life could run out of itself, then, again, we would see there would be a breakdown somewhere in the fabric of the universe, and the whole thing would break apart. But that is not what happens. So if the substance of life cannot diminish, and this total substance of your good becomes your careers, your moneys, your loves, and all the

26

things that support you, if it cannot run out, then if someone or a favored person, place or thing leaves us, we do not have to despair because we know: "I am one with the substance of life that never runs out. It is just shifting to supply via a new channel." The channels and the forms through which this ever-present good is experienced may switch and change, but the substance is ever continual and ever supplying each and all…perfectly according to the life needs of the moment.

Thus, there needs to be a complete change of reference to unfold the power of the glorious Truth of your life, and when you really get this concept and understand that this is the Truth of being, you will stop running out of your good. No more will notions of beginnings and endings trouble you, yet you will find the greatest balm and comfort in the knowing of an Eternal Supply of every form imaginable ever being yours.

Does anyone know those void times? Those vacuum times? They will now dissolve and disappear before your very eyes, for your mind will only know: "I am one with the complete movement of the Substance of Spirit showing up as my good, as I conceive of it at any given time. Therefore, I am never dependent upon any particular person, place or thing." This is the meaning of "God is my Source." This is so great a Principle to know and realize. "The substance of life cannot diminish or run out, and neither can I", for this would constitute lack, right? Another word for death is lack.

Another word for death is failure. If life itself is self-renewing, if spirit is self-renewing, then your ever-ongoing jobs, for example, are the endless avenues for creative self-expression. The right ideas, all that you require, all that is the Substance of God made manifest for you, can never run out and shall be ever present."

Well, if your supply is not running out, then what is it doing? It is renewing, it is renewing. It is changing forms. It is flowing. It is happening right where you are ~ happening for you ~ in different shapes and different configurations. Thus living the Immortal life ~ the consciousness of the Immortal life ~ is living the Truth of never ending expansion and joy. Do you see how this goes together? We didn't say mortal or imperfect substance. We said Immortal substance, and Living the Immortal Life means living the Eternal Truth of never-ending substance for every need. These are the ideas that constitute the "life more abundant" that is talked about by Jesus. "I have come to give you the life more abundant." And this life gets transmitted through contemplating right ideas ~ through correcting your ideas about life, through realizing Perfect Spirit within.

These ideas are the breath of life, and they are the living Substance of Spirit that changes your experience. This also means as well, when we say there needs to be no void, no vacuum, and that we can get well...that each can manifest whatever it is that he or she is wanting without limit, and at the peak of Divine Realization, that which anyone requires now is manifest instantaneously. As you

28

remove ideas of limitation, denial, lack or stagnation, then you may experience your renewal instantaneously. It just really depends upon how fast you can change your mind and your heart about a thing as to how quickly you will renew. No time is imposed upon you.

Say to yourself often when you are meditating, when you get very quiet and you are communing with the Light of your being, centered in the Citadel of all Divine Presence and Power within, say to yourself, "My body, my entire being is composed of the Immortal atoms of God." And let that flow through you and have its meaning for you. Let those profound words have their chemical alchemy, re-ordering all in your physical world. Have the change.

Affirm, "My body is composed of the Immortal atoms of God, atoms of Infinite Divine Light." See what happens to you. "My life is the Immortal Life of God, ever self-renewing in its every aspect." See what happens to you.

We have only just begun, now, as a collective, to tap the consciousness of the magnitude of being that we are. We have only just begun, but we've got a great road that we are on. On the super Highway of God, the possibilities of evolution and expansion for us are endless in this understanding, "I am one with Immortal Life ~ the life of God."

And if we can only grasp this formidable reality, everything will change to become remarkably better at once. Remember to build this Truth into your being now. In other words, grasp it. Remind yourself often. Every time you see yourself thinking in terms of, "Well, I'll never have it…that good again," just remind yourself, you have only begun to experience the greatness. Say to yourself, "There is not a bit of truth in that. I am one." "I am one with the Immortal Life of God. I always have ever-renewing good. That idea of limitation is no idea for me." Reject it. Monitor your own minds. Realize the Infinite avenues of Self-Expression that lie before you. Every atom of the universe supports you in your quest.

Watch your own minds, and from the High Place, where you have the all-power of correction, just change the information that you are giving yourself from untrue to celebrate the lustrous Truth.

If we can grasp some part of this now, just a small part of it, we shall begin to express it in our every moment of expression. The nurturing substance of our elevated thought shall filter in and throughout our being, extending and empowering our lives, bringing more beauty, more creativity, more joy. We shall now begin to cease this pattern of useless aging and dying through separation from the power plant of our life. And begin to treasure and project our eternality. Be a beacon in our everyday living.

I'll just tell you this story before I close this chapter. This has tremendous, tremendous import for you and what the quality of your life will be, and will begin to govern and change your reactions to life and things that happen to and for you. On one occasion, I was out to dinner with my family, and my brother's son. My brother's name is Joel; I call him Jewel), so we are having dinner, and we are having a conversation, and I don't know how it came up, but we were talking about how long we planned to live. And so I was saying to little Joel, my brother's son: "You know, Joel, in the ancient days, people used to live to be like a thousand years. That's what they say. You know, Methuselah?" And his comment to me was, already filled with collective negation, he said, "That's not true."

We then talked some more about it, and he began to open up about the concept...just playfully talking about it. And he asks, "Well, you know, if that is so, how can that ever be possible?" I said, "Well, gee, I don't know. Maybe they used to take better care of themselves. Maybe they used to be happier, and because of that, they would live life much longer." He says, "Yeah. That makes sense."

So by the end of the conversation, I am saying, "Now, Joel, how long are you planning to live?" And he says, "Oh... 200 years." I said, "Boy. That is a really great idea!"

Now look at that consciousness he arrived at, as the Spirit of Truth caused a deep realization in his soul and the light of Divine Inspiration ignited his thought, just as a result of a playful conversation.

31

But I knew when I first started talking with him that already he was conditioned by prevailing beliefs and feeding the limitation. His mind was closed. As young as he was, with the entire universe of possibilities before him, he was already mired in a mind-set, simply thinking what he always heard was so.

So I was kind of lifting him out lightly. But already, by the end of the conversation, he was on a different pattern. And that will have an effect. Sometime he is going to be remembering, when Reverend Linda told him about Methuselah. The Truth shall be there for him just when he needs.

The point is, is this our mind? Do we believe so little in the power of life that we have shortened and disempowered God's life in us so much that we have narrowed life down to: Well, we are lucky if we live thirty, forty or fifty years? Have we narrowed life and the great power that is the power of our life down so much to believe this? If this is us, any one of us, or if in any department of our mind we are clinging to these old defeatist notions, let us stop doing that, and live at the summit of consciousness, where infinite horizons lay before us and all good is possible. And let us be the first ones. Because somebody has always got to lead the show and point the way to a greater destiny for us all.

Let us get a better idea about ourselves. We'll be so much happier, healthier and richer...knowing we are ever one with the

Most High, inheritors of the Divine and Immortal Light, the substance for all good. Let us agree that it is a very exciting idea to have greater potentials and possibilities for ourselves.

Noted mystic and author, Leonard Orr, whose writing is devoted to the study of the ways of the ancient Yogis and Masters, together with the Principles of Immortal life, came to the profound realization of this very Truth, and his suggestion is that you start planning to live eternally now. Honored to have significant personal time with some of the greatest mystics of the Far East, he came to understand the power within, and we all have heard about the phenomenal states of physical mastery that some have attained, yet, perhaps not really grasped that this is the fundamental Truth of our very own existence. We think, "Wow. Look at that one. Yogananda maintained his body for six months. It didn't deteriorate." Realize that state of Grace was the manifestation of his risen consciousness

.Indeed, a living example is herein provided, showing the Truth that consciousness in charge. But better to know that you, in potential, are just like Yogananda and every other Master that exists. As Jesus said: "Do what I do and do it moreso!"

Start planning to live eternally now, that you too may reap the benefits of the Kingdom. Dwell upon the Great Reality and daily plan the most constructive future you can think of. You are going to live eternally anyway, with or without this body.

Build ultimate Truth into your living now, in all things large and small, both every-day and blockbusting. Release those pacts with death, thinking, "I've got to die" at a certain time. "That is all I can do. That's the best I can do." Start to really heal these devastating and limiting notions. Don't leave it for the Buddha. The Buddha's waiting for you to do it now. He wants company, OK?

Plan to express ever more and more Truth and radiance of the Divine Nature, in, through and as yourself. Declare: "I am renewing every moment" and you shall build up a formidable fortress of consciousness. Establish a new Divine Pattern for yourself. Your God genes and cells will be jumping for joy. Believe me. You haven't been talking to them for such a long time, in the words of Truth and Light they know to be so.

Remember: "I am Immortal Spirit, as Immortal now as I ever shall be."

Practice living from this lustrous Truth, and live graciously, and bring in the consciousness of your Immortality now. No matter what you may be going through, center in the Truth.

Always remember: "There is no reason ~ there is no God-reason for me to be sick, to be limited, to age, to be doomed to failure, for I am one with ever-new Spirit." "I am one with that which knows the certain path of victory for me."

34

I celebrate and rejoice in the Divine Life that you are and that I am, and the limitless possibilities of unbounded good that lay before us all.

In closing this chapter, and before we embark on some helpful tools to evolve consciousness and to transform, let us just do a short meditation now to incorporate this Truth, Know that we are starting right now to form this permanent new foundation, and incorporating it in our approach to everything. And who knows what great things we'll be doing, and how much our lives shall change?!!!

LIVING YOUR IMMORTALITY NOW

So let each get very still, breathing in and out the Immortal Elixir of the Divine Breath, going within to the sacred, secret place of the Most High... One now with the brilliant, radiant atom and action of God.... At the Highest High.... At the summit and the peak of Being, we are now radiating North, South, East and West with our consciousness of Divine Life. We are enfolded in our Light Bodies, Divine Patterns of unique Perfection, each and all.

Let us each step up now... Rise up now out of the body shell into the Holy and powerful and radiant, brilliant nucleus of light that is the Light of our being, allowing it to permeate and radiate through our every pore and atom and cell, now immersing in the splendor of the all-encompassing Light.

35

Every aspect of your being is now existing on every level and dimension in the pure Light of Spirit, the very foundation of your life, rich in unlimited, nurturing, healing Light.

And now, let us breathe this light into our being, knowing "This wonderful, all-encompassing Light, rich in all healing capacity is mine."

And now, let each step out again to overview his or her life and see from the High Place, asking:

"Is there anywhere I am putting up with less? Is there anywhere I am putting up with death, failure, defeat, loss, grief? Any area of sadness that needs my perfect knowing of the truth now? Any area that needs my pure consciousness of Immortality?" Note the areas of most major concern that are now revealed to you.

And let each now go with love to that area we seek to heal and that needs to be blessed with our new knowing now, and spread our love and the light of our knowing... Our perfect knowing all around ~ in, around and through this situation.

And we say within, "I am the Projection and the Perfection of Divine Love without ceasing. I am the radiant projection and manifestation of Divine Life, abounding over, in, around and through. All is perfectly renewed now and very well.

36

Thank-you… sublime God of my being for reminding me who I am. Thank-you for the manifestation of my eternal wholeness and joy right here in this area of renewal right now. And we see ourselves now blossoming anew, rising anew, radiant and joyous. And it's so wonderful to be ever so complete.

And so it is.

Know that your word is your instrument of creation. And, as you read the following treatment, allow its content to absorb within your soul, as you speak it silently or out loud.

Enjoy this special excerpt from Songs of Eternity ~ Contemplations, Treatments and Meditations on the Word of God. Refer to it often, any time you need to refresh yourself in the elixir and healing balm of perfect Truth.

~

"LIVING YOUR IMMORTALITY NOW"
"I am Immortal Principle of God."
(THE PRINCIPLE)

Beloved:

The Truth of your being is that you are the Immortal Life of God ~ expressing in space and time and throughout the many mansions of the Kingdom. There is no other Truth.

When you embrace in your heart the Truth of your eternal, ever-on-going existence, as the *Light of God*...And when you live this Truth in your daily affairs ~ limitations, disease, age, suffering and even death itself and all forms of failure dissolve in the blissful Truth of life everlasting; and only radiant life is found.

I am Spirit, and I am Law. I am the life ever expressing. Death, denial, lack, limitation and disease have no power over me.

MEDITATION

(For Contemplating Silently or Out Loud)

"LIVING YOUR IMMORTALITY NOW"

I AM THAT I AM!

AND RIGHT NOW I DECLARE
I AM ONE WITH PERFECT SUBSTANCE DIVINE!
THERE IS NO PAST, NOR FUTURE ~ NOR TIME, NOR SPACE
NOR EXPERIENCE, NOR HISTORY
THAT CAN HOLD ME IN CAPTIVITY...
FOR I AM BORN OF HEAVEN'S MIND
AND I BURN-UP ALL DROSS IN THE FIERY FLAME OF MY
BEING AS I GO!

I AM THE BREATH OF IMMORTAL SPIRIT...
LIVING IN THE ONE-GOD-DAY THAT FLOWS
THROUGHOUT ETERNITY!

THE EVER SELF-RENEWING ACTION OF SPIRIT ~
I STAND FOREVER RADIANT AND FREE!

I AM THE DIVINE VISITOR BROUGHT FORTH
INTO THE EXPERIENCES OF THE DAY ~
ALWAYS KNOWING WHEN TO ARRIVE AND
WHEN TO DEPART.

I LEAVE BLAZES OF BLESSINGS BEHIND ME!

I AM THE DIVINE PATTERN MADE MANIFEST...
KNOWING NO BIRTH, NOR DEATH, NOR DECAY NOR
SIGHS OF MORTALITY.

I AM THE PERFECT CONTINUITY OF SUBLIME LIFE EVER-
UNFOLDING...
INTO NEVER-ENDING BLISS!

I AM ONE WITH ALL THE AGES
AND ALL SPHERES AND DIMENSIONS OF BEING!

~

I ENFOLD ALL IN MY HEART'S EMBRACE RIGHT NOW!
AS I DO, I ENRICH ALL AROUND ME!

I COMMAND MYSELF RIGHT NOW FREE
OF ALL ENCUMBRANCES AND WEIGHTS...
THAT I MIGHT HAVE ATTACHED TO ME!

I AM FREE TO SOAR AND SO I AM THE MIGHTY MAJESTIC
SUCCESS OF GOD ~
COME TO FULLEST EXPRESSION RIGHT WHERE I DESIRE!

THE UNSTOPPABLE POWER, THE IRREPRESSIBLE GLORY...
AND THE RESPLENDENT VICTORY OF GOD-BEING IS MINE
~ RIGHT NOW!

~ AND SO IT IS!

~

Now let us move on to see what we may do to attain and
maintain this most desirable state of being, and successfully maintain
in all our ways.

IMMORTALITY NOW AND FOREVER ~

HOW TO LIVE FOREVER IN YOUR DIVINE BODY OF LIGHT!

CHAPTER TWO

PART I

HOW TO LIVE FOREVER IN YOUR DIVINE BODY OF LIGHT!
~
"BE YE TRANSFORMED"
THE GOLDEN PATHWAY TO SPIRITUAL, MENTAL, PHYSICAL EVOLUTION!

CHAPTER TWO

Part I

HOW TO LIVE FOREVER ~ IN YOUR DIVINE BODY OF LIGHT!

"Be Ye Transformed!"

Our chapter title is very special and significant ~ "How to Life Forever in Your Divine Body of Light", and I am not kidding. And... here we are not talking how to live with death. We are talking about the possibility of each of us completely transcending that idea, and eliminating the idea of death and dying completely from the collective psyche. This takes a lot of realization of the ultimate Truth of who and what we really are.

Once, there was a very great speaker by the name of Jim Morrison who used to give a talk at Carnegie Hall and his title was "How to Live Forever, In the Body ~ You Walked Into Carnegie Hall In!". Though this was a while ago, he drew a very great crowd… for such a statement indeed stirs the knowing of the Truth of the possibility of this evolutionary manifestation deep within us all.

So just to give you an overview before we get into how each could accomplish this glorious transcendent way of being, along with possible ways to accomplish this task… realize that profound changes have already been occurring, ever since the time of the Great Alignment of the planets.

I shall never forget that stunning singular moment, when I traveled with friends from busy Los Angeles to the depths of the stark Mohave Desert in the middle of the night to witness the bright streak of light, as the heavenly comet shot across the dark, night skies ~ lighting up all in its gaze.

From that period on, there has continued to be great evolutionary change ~ and whether we are looking within at the quality of our very own lives or without at the movement of the heavenly spheres, realize it is all one thing happening. Whether we look at this alignment as an external phenomena only, or as a representative of that which is happening within our own collective consciousness, or whether you believe in external causation, i.e. "It's the planetary alignment that did it"… really ~ what it all is and what it comes down to 'is', that all things of heaven and earth have been working together and coming together…for all humanity to achieve this ultra- awareness of who and what we are, and "As within, so without!"

At the time of this alignment, a powerful new surge of consciousness began and started this new movement towards the realization of the Higher in us all ~ providing the thrust toward a whole new dimension of life experience and from that point on, the collective mind has been working more and more together. You'll notice that every year, there are peace gatherings, where spiritual consciousness is being nurtured. I can't say reborn, because the awareness of the Spiritual Reality of our being has always been, but in the Golden Age of the New Millennium, greater awareness is really coming to the fore together with all of the ideas that go along with a true Spiritual Consciousness.

This lustrous movement is happening through each and every one of us, each feeling this motivation to come into a greater understanding of who we are as Divine Beings and what our possibilities and potentials are.

Groups of like-minded souls continue to meet all over the world and what we are talking about isn't a new idea, but up until this time, the knowing of our Immortal Essence has been kind of reserved for the secret holy places. And you will see that this greater awareness is going to become more and more pervasive, as even our great metaphysicians in all professions, including doctors and scientists are talking about this phenomena right now, understanding that the power of consciousness and Faith is mighty indeed.

Thus, since the time of the Great Alignment, depicting our evolutionary move, Truth has been coming up to the surface of our collective minds from deep below, the knowing of who we are rising up from all the buried resources of our consciousness, of our buried storehouse of memory… something like Atlantis coming up from the sea, the Secrets of the Ages have been coming up in our minds.

Now, it is very interesting ~ the second phenomena of the comet hitting Jupiter out-pictured on a symbolic level another arrangement of the heavenly bodies taking place, another adjustment of Highest Mind. And mythologically speaking, Jupiter represents the energy of Love and Wisdom. Whenever there is alignment of a heavenly body with our planetary home, it is good to look within and ask: "What is the Spiritual Light Essence and Consciousness of this energy? What influx and assistance in advancement can it mean for me?

Higher Awareness has been coming to the fore in ever-increasing waves of true enlightenment ever since these two mighty configurations, and our collective consciousness has become sufficiently heightened to know that in order to advance any further, we need a lot more Love, we need a lot more Wisdom, and we need to incorporate the Higher Awareness of who and what we are.

45

With this picture in mind of what has been happening on the collective level, you can grab hold and implement in your own life with greater clarity and commitment, for if you have felt rumblings within yourself, compelling to rise Higher, but you are not really aware of what is happening or have no Divine Pattern or model in mind, it is hard to connect yourself into that mighty stream and current of Higher Awareness, that is compelling from within.

The following is an exceptional statement of the Great Reality that was written by Dr. Erwin Seale, who was one of the original contributors to the profound understanding of the Science of Mind, the teaching evolved by very advanced minds of illumined awareness, a very great mind, as was Fillmore and Holmes.

Contemplation upon his mighty words will lead you into awareness of your Immortal Self, so just take a moment to absorb the meaning of his profound words, and we will proceed from there.

"Man is Divine, and man/woman is free. We were not born, nor shall we die. He is, God is spirit and cannot be contained in any form or imprisoned in any condition. The true self, the Atman cannot be hurt, is never healed, is complete and whole already. It is not in prison. Atman can never be defeated, cannot be deprived of any good or stricken with any grief. Atman has no enemy, therefore does not fight and is never beaten… Wins in all its ways by its pure being-ness.

It is always and ever serene and at peace, and rides above the fogs and damps of the earth in undiminished joy. The Divine Self is sinless, healthy, perfect, whole and free, without care, knowing no fear. Nothing can be added unto the perfection that it is and nothing can be taken from it. It is whole, ever whole, sound, complete and totally self-sustained."

"That thou art, I am".

And, this profound understanding of the center of the life of the human being has been recognized by all great yogis and Masters from the beginning of time ~ ever the same, whether ancient or modern. So needless to say, what we are talking about is the nature of the one Divine Self, that lives and breathes in every human being, and bringing the capacities and energies of our Divine Self to the fore.

Our glorious purpose now is to evolve, to come a step forward past any level of awareness that we have ever known, and literally our purpose is to change right now our understanding of who we are, at the most fundamental level of heart and soul, and to understand the merits of the Immortal Life that is ours.

Every hope of our progression and our perfect evolution depends on establishing this initial point of reference. For without this greater alignment, there is no greater horizon to aspire to.

47

Either we are identifying with the totality of spirit and all that it is as "all that we are", or we are not. There is no in-between.

And any idea in between this, anywhere where we are straddling the line, dooms us to repeat our past, to repetition on that karmic wheel of dying and being born again and dying and being born again.

So what are we? is the ultimate question to really ask, and this question brings forward empowering information for your soul. At some point, each one of us has to know again, re- know what we are, shed all notions of false beliefs, re-recognize and accept the higher revelation right into our physical life and all our activities right now, walking the talk in all our ways.

What are we really from the Divine Point of view? Plumbing the depths of this question, the realization dawns: We are the thought of God, the perfect individualization of God made manifest without any division whatsoever. The thought of God made manifest. There is no reality to separation from the Divine Cause to all of life. There is no spirit and matter. There are no two things. There is only one thing. Only 100% spiritual forms of Divine measure and 100% Divine Substance. That is all there is. And our potential experience of good and freedom rests in our conscious recognition and embodiment of this undying Truth, as we go along, ever deeper, ever Higher, unto limitless horizons in our embodiment of this fact.

Thus, the very first point and number one task to achieve is to realize that unless we really consciously incorporate this Truth of being and speak our word, with no embarrassment and no apology, we cannot rise to benefit from the bountiful fruits of the Kingdom. Unless we realize that we are 100% spiritual, we cannot make the leap into the next dimension of Higher Experience, always awaiting our recognition.

Secondly, realize each of us is endowed with free will, and right of choice as to which path we will follow. The Divine Being-ness created us "as it is" with freedom to choose our destinies, for what good would it be to have a bunch of people coming home to the Kingdom again, who were forced home. Ask yourself... which path will prosper you most?

So the whole thing that we are about is making our conscious evolution of recognizing who we are, and bringing it out in all our ways and beliefs. In so doing, we live the life of ever greater portions; and we have the free will to choose identification with our mortality and with our limitations, or to identify with Infinite Source, and I am sure that each one reading has had some experience of improvement in your life through identification with Source or Infinite God or Great I am, the great Truth of your being. Every time you do that, don't you transcend your experience, and don't you arrive at a different level? Aren't you adorned with success beyond any measure of the past?

49

Thus it is that clinging to old, limited beliefs dooms the individual to fixed experiences of repetition, shutting out the Great Light of the Spiritual Sun. We don't get out. It is like going around and around in circles. Limited materialistic thinking binds us to that karmic wheel, while the greater choice provides a straight line upward into further dimensions of bliss.

Expanding consciousness of one's Eternal Reality raises the individual completely, as we can see with Christ and any other great Master, who perfected their consciousness, meaning their understanding of who they are in God, indeed a Divine son or daughter of the Most High. When we introduce the Divine factor, we become raised in all that we do, uplifting all in our earth experience and beyond. In every domain we excel. Such is the Power of the Kingdom within, rich in transcendent ways and means, as we know with certainty there is nothing that cannot be overcome and healed in perfection by the Greater- in-me.

And the great thing about God-inclusion in your consciousness is that your level of excelling now becomes so much more empowering and beneficial than anything you could ever accomplish, while in your thoughts of separation. Aligned with Divine Spirit, no negative consequences attach.

So, the big question is: "What's the big deal, why resist? What good can it bring to continue on the path of denial and defeat?

Rather, let us see how great it is to live in the consciousness of the Allness, and do all we can to align ourselves with Divine Principle.

Civilization has now completed a 2000-year cycle that started with the Manifestation of Jesus. Son of the Father, the radiant Christ laid out the perfect pattern of evolution for each and all, including ascension, letting you know that the seed of God-potential rests within each and every one. In all his miracles, he showed mankind's original regal relationship with the Divine, and it has been through him and his radiant life, gracing the face of humanity ~ that we have learned the Great Truth of our very own Divine selves. This glowing pattern of ultimate being has remained imprinted within our collective soul, and we have been slowly evolving over time, now coming to the glorious time when all is right and perfect to realize the more, to perfect our understanding, and to bring out these lustrous Higher patterns, through our very being, the great idea.

For a while, civilization had slipped very far down. Remember in the dark ages, society as a whole forgot who we really are, and things got pretty intense, as persons slowly forgot God, forgot all of the immeasurable gifts, resulting in a lowering of the entire consciousness and suppression of Highest Awareness. But now we have been and continue to be on the ascending cycle, which means an awakening cycle or an evolution upward and outward. All things are going home, so to speak in the sense of consciousness, and you want to benefit as much as you can.

There is no limit as to how far each can go, in realizing the Divine Presence and Power of life that ever stands available to all. Now we are moving out of the third dimension into a fourth dimensional experience, and the ingredient that is different about the fourth dimensional experience, providing the helium of ascent, is that this is the level of being, where the human being now becomes rich in Awareness of his or her true Spiritual Identity, and his or her life becomes greatly blessed and expanded by the inclusion of God. Otherwise, one will continue to run around in the pattern of third dimensional experience, which means never getting out, until you finally choose to make the greater quantum leap of understanding the nature of Unlimited Divine Beingness as you.

Thus, the thrust is to break through into fourth dimensional experience, which is the God-dimension.

And so it is that, as a collective, we are moving on the whole to greater inclusion of Atman, God-man and God-woman, no longer God and man, but God in man, as man, through man, one thing, God-man, "Atman" ~ not two, not God and man or spirit and matter.

As each re-accepts God and all that is sublime into our physical, emotional, mental systems, what is happening is an awakening of the total memory of our Divine Origins, bit by bit, along with everything that is contained in that Divine Memory, which is always existent. We just have been so encumbered, so bogged down that we haven't been able to see it, and now we are getting the glimmers and so the benefits of this Highest Realization ~ "My life is God's Life"... is nothing that we are going outside ourselves to get. It is already resident, a seed of Divine potential forever and already existent within each and every one.

Rest assured that as a collective, we are moving to this greater estate of being and awareness, and if you have attended some of the great gatherings of great metaphysicians from around the world and all branches of the sciences and arts, where several hundred or thousands have come together in celebration of Truth, you can see without doubt, without question, what is happening and these minds are on fire with the Truth. They are lit up with the Truth and with this rediscovery and re-immersion in the radiant Truth of Being, so enlivening to the Soul.

Thus it is that in this lustrous time, we are having an awakening of our total Divine Memory, as we align ourselves with Principles of Spiritual Essence. Our Divine memory is opening wide. And what is happening simultaneously is that there is a total Spiritualization simultaneously of our body forms.

Our bodies form anew and heal, as we merge with the Higher Self... and the Higher Self may be regarded as Atman already. Each already has his or her Divine Form, the Divine Pattern within, but we don't experience it, until we talk its language. On every level of manifest life ~ Physically, mentally, and emotionally, everything responds to Spirit and what Spirit is knowing to be true. So how do you come to place where you do not even have to visit your plastic surgeon for improvement? By the inclusion of limitless Divine Principle, always regenerating in you, and that alone removes and corrects whatever needs correction within your body. The rose is in the seed, and there are no two things or two causes to being. Remember now we are saying there is only thing. There cannot be spirit and then body, having nothing to do with spirit.

Body is the reflection of spirit, the reflection of the activity of your consciousness. What your mind is on is what your face shows, the great Emerson said. Realize this is the Law of your being. There is no other Law that has ever been instated in the universe, or that holds sway as some other law of your being and/or existence.

Thus, let us stretch our sights to say and to deeply cognize, that there is a total spiritualization of every form of life going on and of your own physical form, not that it never was not always of *Spiritual Essence*, yet our conscious recognition is bringing this glowing Truth into the light of day, emerging, as the butterfly from the chrysalis, as the radiant Light from behind the clouds.

And so ~ as we perfect our knowing now in this stage called the fourth dimension, we are not leaving our bodies behind us.

Rather, we are simply bringing in more Light, revealing the perfect Divine Light Pattern within, applying the Perfect Healing Truth.

You can rest assured that you are not going to suddenly take off the planet, if you get into Divine Ideas of the great "What Is" ~ and you are not losing your body, rather, you are just becoming more and more your Divine Body of Light. Leaving the body behind would not be completing the task. The idea is to reflect through the body condition the Perfection of Spirit, the wholeness of the Divine Self. For the body is the mere mirror reflector of our thinking and knowing patterns and nothing else. All is One and there is only one thing, can you see how this is? This deep Truth that body follows and reflects consciousness is something for you to deeply contemplate on, if you can't quite cognize that. Consciousness is always in charge. There is no will, nor power in body of itself.

Our thinking and knowing patterns form an atomic gravitational magnetic field. Whatever one's mind is on produces an atomic field that draws molecular substance and forms the body or physical pattern. This magnetic field then becomes the form of what we are thinking about. Realize how magnetic you are. Through the center of your being which is consciousness, you continuously draw the molecules in and they are literally held in shape and particular form through the pictures in your consciousness. Now on a very basic level you can see how it is. Haven't you often said: "Today I feel great", and then suddenly there is a different appearance to you.

55

There is a lightening up of even the skin when you are happy. There is continuous molecular activity going on through you. You are literally shaping your body and your destiny through the quality of your thoughts, so keep your thoughts on High and filled with Divine Life and awareness of the Presence ever at hand. You are the one, shaping your body at every moment.

Realize that this activity is always going on, as thoughts form our worlds ~ that we are magnetic centers, and through the substance of our thoughts we ever-create our manifest world. Realize that thoughts and resultant forms are malleable. People can lose weight, perfect their looks, and can heal the emotional life, through perfecting their temperament. The age of God-man is upon us. Atman is arriving, the new race, the Divine Idea of God, the Spiritual Idea is being realized through Atman, which is us, which is our Higher Self, which is ever one with God. Through our Higher Selves, we can see ourselves on this ever-ascending journey now, even as we struggle in the world, knowing we shall overcome through the Highest and the Best in ourselves. Choose to be ever on an ascending cycle, no more in a decline. Rejoice in taking the blinders off. Know you are on an ascending cycle, where you can fully succeed, now empowered to cast off and release death.

Now, the necessity of releasing ideas of death, dying and decay must be pretty obvious, even if you look at it just from an intellectual point of view. How can you possibly move up if you are hanging on to death and/or defeat? It just doesn't make sense, does it? Yet, each can transcend now, as far as can be conceived, and in the buoyancy of this cycle, spirit is guiding us and helping us to open up all that we need to know and realize about the greatness of Spirit within. Thus, in order for us to get onto this Higher Level of Livingness, it is essential to start living from a consciousness of our Immortality and a realization that death is not necessary. We can have it, if we want it, but death is not an idea that was born of Spirit. How could it be? If there were anything in Spirit that propelled things toward death, this universe would be non-existent. Know and affirm; "There is only one thing and that is life force, moving through all and all that is life and perpetuating it eternally."

Now because of our free will, we can choose to let our body breakdown, our machinery, our earthy equipment. We can die the body off, take a brief respite, then try it again. But the point is we don't have to do that anymore. So I am not saying that you have to go for the whole apple, but if you do, you will extend your life much further than anyone else. And you want to realize that you alone are in charge of your body and taking care of it by maintaining highest thoughts, projections, feelings, and awareness…realizing indeed, it is the living Temple of the Most High.

Ultimately, it is the choice of the Divine Soul within as to how long one shall maintain body and find earth experience of value. And when one goes from our sight, let us acknowledge that one just made his or her transition into the Greater, taking the word "death" entirely out of our vocabulary.

Yes, it is a choice. We don't realize that the subconscious mind sets out life goals and programs out the life, and once it gets infilled with certain concepts, these concepts begin to govern one's every outcome. Now if you've been hearing about you are going to age or you are going to die, you are going to this and that, if you have been hearing about that since the time that you came into this plane, it is going into your subconscious and your patterning and you are living out that decree that in fact you made temporarily true for yourself…by your unquestioned acceptance.

Yet, on the other hand, some individuals live a very great and risen life and they decide at a certain point; "I have accomplished my every good purpose and I now want to release this body", and so they let the material body go so to speak, just like an old suit of clothing which one would take off in favor of donning a better suit.

Try to think of all being totally your choice, knowing you will fulfill your every aspiration that you have come to fulfill, and the body is your vehicle of operation on this plane, filled with all the life and ever-renewing power of Spirit, for as long as you decide.

It never matters how far you are able to manifest the perfection, only that you are ever aware of the possibilities available to you, and daily building the consciousness. Your faithfulness shall prove you true.

You don't want to be compelled by subconscious forces that you have just blindly accepted along the way, yet ever know your body is the Temple of the Most High, rich in all self-healing attributes and powers. That is why we do our conscious work to take out and transform the negative subconscious patterning to reflect the perfect Truth of Infinite and Immortal Being. But, above all, begin to realize consciousness is in charge, and choose how long you want to maintain your physical form always holding the Divine Pattern of perfect healing and self-regeneration before you.

To achieve this High Stage of Fourth Dimensional Awareness, as we have seen great gurus, saints and avatars have done, two things are necessary.

One, the new, complete and conscious identification with the total life and substance of God must be present, because in God, there is no death. In God there is no death, and indeed there never is in the Great Reality of Divine Life. Even if we think we are dying, we are not. We are simply transitioning to a greater stage, birthing into another mansion of existence. So, strive to understand that in God, there is no death. There can only be one thing, and that is radiant and ever-ongoing Life. If there were two powers, it would be something else, but you are free by virtue of your human will to cognize whatever level you choose to hold close to your heart about this fact.

After truly understanding that we need that new relationship and realization of who we are as Immortal Spirit, one with God... then we need to establish a new relationship with the entire cosmos of being by steadily perfecting ourselves in Love and Light, to harmonize ourselves, even as the Creator of *All that Is* loves the entire universe of Creation. If we remain agitated or against anyone or anything, we cannot reach the state of any type of Godliness or perfection, nor touch the Omni-Powers of Divine Love. Understand that earth is the material plane, where life forms and codifies the Substance of Spirit, forms and codifies and densifies and objectifies.

Spirit is creative. Spirit is ever manifested, ever manifesting. It's a natural impulse, so always and ever know that we are a manifestation of Spiritual life, of the invisible things of thought, ever compelling manifestation. To us ~ form is not different from Spirit. Form is simply the visible and tangible place where we witness the stuff of Spirit happening.

Now, mind is all, consciousness is all and consciousness rules earth plane. The human is endowed with the power to change. That is why we can conduct such investigation into Truth, and benefit from all kinds of healing therapies, and realize the Science of Mind, through the penetration of our own Higher Mind into Truth...

This is how we operate change. Consciousness is all. Consciousness rules body. Consciousness rules physical body and body of conditions, so consider this idea... If I depart body, if I take off for a while, will body get up and walk and talk and do things on its own?

We know that it won't, right. What happens to body if I as consciousness depart body? It falls in a heap, right? Okay, exactly. So we must intelligently conclude from this that something else is in-charge of body. And what is that? Silent Spirit, the force of the individual soul within...and also consciousness, mind and consciousness ever move upon the waters of Eternal being.

Body is the mirror of my mind and responds to my thought about it. Body responds to the sum total of my thoughts and feelings, known or unknown. That is why we are trained so specifically in metaphysics to diligently observe the substance and quality of our thoughts, and to be aware of what we are believing to be true.

If we are not looking at ourselves and saying, wonderful, wonderful you and recognizing one's self as the beauty of spirit, the perfection, the all-capacity, then we will be radiating the results of an inferior thought pattern, lurking within and affecting every outcome. Body always reflects to you your thought. Knowing this, how do we heal something? By changing our thought about it... by realizing a greater and more Universal Truth. Realize that body is totally responsive to your level of consciousness, and realize that

Truth is Universal and not just confined to a particular individual or group. All are the limitless and perfect life of God. In this knowing, is there anything that cannot be healed by centering in Truth?

That is the very means by which some great Masters can levitate and perform all the miraculous feats that they do, even controlling their circulatory system. Those who have attained Mastery of the physical plane are in total absolute charge of what is happening because they realize this fact that consciousness rules body and that is the way it is. When you change your consciousness about a body of circumstances, again a manifestation of spirit in form, your material conditions or any experience you have gone through… when you harmonize with that, blessing instead of cursing, forgiving and releasing, your entire body of circumstances change, don't they? So it is that you can heal so wonderfully, when you realize your body is the Temple of the Unlimited and the Divine.

When you convert hate into love and you project that blessing over your circumstance, have you not manifested an entirely new and beneficent relationship with that particular someone or something? We are taught to praise without ceasing, which is an activity of Love. Praise lifts every cell of the being. Praise will increase your bank account, praise alone, without a phone call. Just say, "I praise the wonderful substance of Infinite Life that is. I praise that condition, I praise it into perfect health and well-being, I praise it." And this Divine element of praise has life power within in it always multiplying in goodness and strength the thing that you are praising. So it is very important to understand that consciousness is in-charge of body and we are in charge of our experience.

Praise can lift a failing organ to perfect health. Ever praise the Light and Love of God within, fulfilling you in all your ways.

Though some things seem impossible to achieve in the now, it is not unfamiliar to us to know of individuals who can walk on fiery stones, without being burned. Athletes now soar to unimaginable heights with their skateboards high in the air. Imagine what lays before us, as we realize more and more the Truth of our limitless being.

If one seems to fail in any endeavor, just be humble and realize you have not made it totally yet, pick up the Divine Sword of challenge, and once you have increased consciousness sufficiently to thoroughly transcend, filling with the limitless life and Love of the Creator, as your very own...you will have a healing experience, more beneficent than you have ever known.

Every appearance of infirmity of any sort is an opportunity to rise up in greater realization of the Presence and Power of a greater Divine attribute in you ~ to the tipping point where there are no more impossible(s) to you, where darkness turns to joyous Light, a Divine challenge, as it were. And, in the overcoming you will have released some hidden concept of difficulty, of concern with space and time to realize that to the Divine in You all is easy.

And through coming up over our infirmities of any kind, we can come to another level of well-being through an incorporation of Greater Truth. This is exactly what happens in healing. We conceive of a greater idea about ourselves and true healing happens in a consciousness of Truth, of the Presence and Power of Spirit within.

It is for this very reason, that right at the inception of any difficulty whatsoever, it behooves us to immediately recognize the transcendent power of the Divine within, and claim its operation in the situation, giving thanks daily for the Divine Outcome of immeasurable good sought, right in the midst of the circumstance, focusing only on most beneficent results…no matter what appears. In the consciousness of Immortal Life, we recognize there is always a greater state of being to be attained, that ever awaits to bless us so profoundly, as we persevere in dwelling in only Limitless Truth.

In so doing, we achieve liberty from outer influence of any kind, becoming true Masters of our own destiny in God. For example, let us say I've got a cold and I am thinking "I am just Linda", playing out the collective mind… "Now, it's flu season and it is time to get a cold." Once under the influence of pervading thought, instead of God itself, I am susceptible to everything. I am walking, talking effect, at the mercy of popular trends. But when I realize my dominion in spirit, and everybody else says it's time for cold, I can now say and affirm, "Well, that is not for me" and with such conviction, I can be in a room full of colds, and I will not get even a sniffle. And then, with this knowledge of my true freedom, if I have unintendedly gotten something, I can correct it by knowing the perfect Truth that "There are no colds in God.", and giving thanks that any and all remnants of cold have disappeared.

If I have permitted something to get into my body somehow without knowing, and most of this is without knowing, I can clean it out with the Light of my God-power, from the within. I am not resigned and I do not ever have to resign myself to any condition whatsoever and shortly I am going to give you some methods of how to do this. Most importantly, when you are working through something, remember it doesn't deny the greatness of your consciousness, or your potential whatsoever. You are simply increasing in capacity beyond limitations of the past.

Everything we choose to experience is like an experiment, unconsciously motivated, as the soul chooses certain challenges for your evolution. Let us say for eons, you have repeatedly come into this plane and not felt physically good. You have not been able to care of body as you should -~ not experienced radiant health and are not getting on top of issues of the body, consciousness-wise. So your soul will keep giving you that task until you get the Divine Idea and have arrived at the summit view, where you are in perfect charge, through realization of Highest Truth. When you have a challenge, realize there is absolutely nothing wrong with you. You are a place for Divine Opportunity, and once you realize the Temple of Divine Life that you are, whole, complete and perfect, there will be no more need for the challenges, as your physical well-being will be successfully attained.

There is an underlying, compelling force we feel when we come up against such challenges, and if we came into this plane of existence and everything was gravy, there would be no act of consciousness, there would be no evolution, nor act of spirit discovering itself through us. So the great thing to know is that when you can look at whatever you are going through as a Divine Opportunity to discover that great something you have been seeking to know, and when you get that something of your God-Self, that optimum understanding of the glorious Light that you are, you will have passed your own test so to speak and you will be released from the troublesome condition. It never needs to come again. The Divine Purpose has been achieved.

You don't have to go through the difficulty anymore. That is what is so great about accepting your challenges now, and making friends with it, so to speak. If you are interested in accelerating, say this is a Divine Challenge, it didn't come to defeat me, it came as a signal that my consciousness needs a tuning up. Now where there is problem, there is always a solution. There is a solution, the solution is within you and it is within your Divine Self, the Supreme Knower, resting right within the wholeness of your Divine Pattern, always One with God.

This is a very great thing to know ~ that the perfection already lies within. For, by the Law of Being, we will respond according to our idea about a thing. For example, if you know there is no power in virus, there is only the Health of God, here you are putting your Divine Self back in the driver's seat. Let us take another situation, for example a yogi or anyone for that matter, drinking poison and not knowing there is poison, never having heard of poison... They will not be affected. There are stories of cases of children with cancer and every other kind of so-called terminal conditions, and the doctors were wise enough not to label it and the child not knowing that he or she had a so-called condition, healed themselves automatically.

Truly everything is consciousness. To the innocent, all is Divine. There is only one thing which is Divine Substance, but through our free will and consciousness, we can make any condition an enemy. We can say poison is real, but it is not. It is merely our idea about it, so what is virus? Virus is an idea that people catch. It is not a thing of itself, it is an idea that is caught by people. Now these notions that there are things that can poison us, there are viruses, there are this's and there are that's, are all born out of our sense of duality and that there are two things or powers.

It is the way we objectify our idea of: "There is God, and then there is the other, opposing force." Ask yourself, if you never hear anything about disease, would you experience it?

Try and avoid labeling conditions, fixing them in time and space. If you give the appearance a label, then you are owning it, and this is why metaphysicians say never, never, never get into the labeling game; claiming "I have a this, I have a that".

Simply acknowledge what is going on, and then proceed to claim the Divine Presence and Light right where that condition is, bringing all aright. Seek the limitless Divine Principle that is capable of overcoming, and center in that awareness, letting it flow in and through your every atom and cell of being, healing all in its mighty sweeping motion.

No matter how real a situation seems to be, yet, if you really want to heal, realize there is that power that is so much greater in you, and begin to claim it as the only force, operating through every atom and cell of your being, restoring to perfect health.

No matter what persons say or want to predict for you, keep focus on the Divine Presence, Giving Thanks for your perfect healing, for there is nothing in God that cannot be overcome. Through joining your consciousness with the Most High, the limitless capacity required becomes yours. Daily praise the Divine

Presence and Power in your life. Daily use your sacred tool of vision to contemplate the Great Reality of Limitless healing power, to accelerate in time and space, and to catalyze your future good, by dwelling only in the High Place, asking only: "What is the Divinely Desirable outcome here? Increase your pictures of good, and keep your mind on the Divine Condition you desire to attain, Giving Thanks it is already so. Divine Wisdom provides the way.

Know appearances have no reality of their own, and have come to pass. Know there is only Divine Substance and the awesome power of the Infinite Light. Change your thinking about whatever you may be experiencing, and say there is only Divine Substance and there is no such a thing as virus, for example, nor any power in it, and you will never experience virus. There cannot be two causes to things. There cannot be God and other forces, but we have freedom within to do what we will with our consciousness, and to place our Faith where it benefits us the most.

One wonderful student I was so blessed to work with had a so-called condition of cancer in the marrow of her bones, and, if you were to see her today, you would see what a dynamo of courage and strength she is.

When she first came to me with her issues, she had bought into the fear, the terror of this disease, the whole thing and then everybody putting the labels on and treating it, putting attention on it, making it so, thus giving it a very powerful temporary life. Everything in her life had become about this disease. The fear of not making it past the time the Doctors said she had left was eating away at her every moment.

Her story of ultimate victory has everything to do with the exercise of will, authority. When she and I first worked together and though she was already a great practitioner and a great accomplisher of Truth in her life, the physical challenge she was undergoing appeared to be so very serious that she thought she could never overcome the negative predictions that had been surrounding her, but something in her knew there was greater for her, if only she could know what that was.

She had tried every method available and yet still was trapped in what appeared to be a never-ending cycle of only partially effective treatments, as the condition continued to compound.

One of the first and most primary issues we immediately cleared up is that of the use of her will. And so I had her repeat after me ~ "I will occupy this body so long as I choose until I fulfill my every good purpose." In the instant, she welled up with tears, hardly able to get the words out, as she tried to say, "I will ..." But then she stood up and resolutely said it again, and then she got it, and then she did it, and she indeed was filled with Power to transcend that condition, and that is no more. And she is still doing that.

How powerful is our right of choice, with strong decisions enlivening every healing substance to move into action.

In the moment, she had decided to accept the sword of Divine Challenge and to come above this and her fire of spirit and will to overcome was very great, faithful, loyal and true to the Divine possibility of her total freedom from this condition. As we spoke in depth re: the many causes that might have provoked this condition surfacing, I said, the very first thing you got to do is you've got to stop agreeing and start saying no to any ideas of limitation. You have got to say no to all these fatal predictions and you have got to make a statement to yourself that your body is Divine and cannot know such a thing, only empowering your unlimited, God self within.

"From that point of aligning with the Divine-in-you, you have evicting power to anything lesser than the perfection of Infinite Healing Light-in-action that you are." So, she firmly made her greater spiritual decision to overcome and truly get well.

A huge realization came over me, when treating for her victorious overcoming through the Divine power within her, just as she went in to get a scan of the tissue. While in deep prayer and bringing the Light to this situation and knowing only the Perfect Truth for her of every atom, cell, and tissue of her being...In one stellar moment, I just really, really realized and deeply cognized the

Great Reality that there can be nothing other than perfection, the central core of the Truth of her being, because there is only Divine Substance, the totality of all Love, Light, Wisdom and Know-how.

In the instant, I saw it and I knew it and I really knew it for a fact. This is what I mean about getting into these ideas so profoundly that you really cognize it at a feeling level and then, shortly after this realization, I heard from her, filled with glowing news and just so happy. She in fact called me right from the doctor's office, and said she had gotten 100% clearance, that there was nothing wrong with her. This is after three years of ongoing treatments and bordering on going into full-fledged chemo.

She had made a choice. She was not going into chemo. She was not going to interrupt her progress, by introducing further treatments. She was going to maintain her new found health with Spiritual Awareness, coupled with right diet, meditation and exercise.

So between the two of us, and of course the great agency of God that is available to correct anything, the cancer was corrected, eliminated, converted and dissolved, every cell converting to be the Love and Life of God.

Now, if she had not evinced such total commitment, perhaps she would have still needed the assistance of further treatments along the pathway of ultimate emancipation, and, if she still needed assistance, she certainly would have done any and all things recommended.

There are so many dynamics involved in such a profound healing, and one must have cultivated such a certain and strong consciousness within, grounded in Divine Light and awareness of the superior capacities already within you, to experience such wonderful results, but the bottom line factor to any profound healing is the realization that there is only God. Yet, society has been replete with fear, terrorizing you.

Don't you think that if I can keep you distracted by diseases and all types of things, you'll never know who you are, never!... and never rise into the perfect Divine Pattern of Health that you can always be. The negative force of collective mind is insidious, it keeps trying to have its own power, and people don't even know they are engaging in limited thought, nor falling under its influence. Rather, keep your consciousness on the attributes of the Divine Self, and learn to rely upon this all-capacity for all your needs. Think of yourself gaining more and more Infinite Health and well-being daily, with no end in sight as to how much well-being you can achieve.

You have the great and sacred tool of forgiveness, to set yourself free of any erroneous and limited ideas you have accepted as true. Forgive yourself and all others who may have played a part

73

in lowering your consciousness, thus, your vision of the future for yourself. Live in the Eternal Now, praising your inherent capacity to ever-ascend and transcend more and more limitation.

For the sake of keeping your emotional body clear and filled with Light, "Forgive them, for they know not what they do", and move on your merry way. Do not get stuck in any limitation notion, believing it is true. You are either being a vessel to play out the record of the prevailing collective mind opinion and absorbing every new limitation idea persons come up with, or you are being an individualization of God and being who you are and taking your stand, okay.

And so, it was that identification with God, the Highest and the Best in herself, and realizing there is only one substance, and there isn't any enduring Truth to anything else, brought this wonderful woman total emancipation.

But if we believe that conditions are an actual power of their own, we will play it out like a play, like a dream, with the veil the Maya of delusion covering over the beautiful, Immortal Divine Self.

Believing in the notion of limitation is an illusion, the grand illusion that masks the glowing Truth. Yet, we indeed do have the right of our illusions, so long as we wish to indulge in them and give them power.

Strive to always remember that these two primary changes are necessary, a new identification with the complete life and substance of God, and nothing else; and watch your mind. The instant find yourself you saying, "Oh virus is going around", simply take a deep breath and re-affirm the perfect Truth: "There is only one thing going around that I am catching and that is God, that is the only thing I catch, and the only substance I am vulnerable to." And secondly, understand that your consciousness is in charge, there is no power in things out there. Just as there is no power in conditions, there is not an iota of power in virus or anything else. It is not a thing on its own. Conditions only have life, if you give them life, how? By means of your consciousness. That is how the life force and all manifestation works for us...through our conscious recognition, acceptance and most deeply held visions and beliefs.

If I say, "Oh this might be real" and "This condition is such a great problem that I will never be able to overcome", forgetting my Divine Self and all the power that is truly within, in that moment ~ my whole being and everything around me will begin to act out my thought, but it doesn't make it an Eternal Truth.

Unwanted conditions are just a manifestation of my freedom that allows me to bump my head against the wall as many times as I want, until one day the ceiling lifts and I glimpse the Truth and I recognize it and I say: "Enough of this already. There is so much more to me."

So for all things physical, including body of external conditions, now we know there is only consciousness in-charge of body and in-charge of conditions. Consciousness, consciousness... thus, we see everything is changeable, everything is malleable. Life cannot be fixed, like Dr. Seale said. Life cannot be fixed to any routine, including death, dying or any cycle because life is life ~ 100% life. That is all it is and it goes on, perpetuating itself forever, utilizing whatever appropriate means.

Life is a manifestation of God, rich in such glorious life-sustaining attributes we have yet to discover. And, the life force goes on of its Self, regardless of human opinion.

Life is God, God is life, God is good, and goes on eternally. Whether you are joining up with the mighty stream or not, it is just going to keep going and produces another body for you, if you didn't do so hot in the one you are in, okay. So maximize your good opportunities to embrace the Truth and live the life abundant in the now. For wherever you go, there you are ~ the sum total of all the realizations, experiences and good habits of consciousness you have established. Go as far as you can, incorporating the lustrous Truths of your eternal being in God in your every area of concern, that the sunshine of Victory may be yours.

On every level, from the fine etheric to the dense physical ~ everything has form. And, you will never be without form. Now the form may change and refine from the dense physical level to a radiant Divine Pattern of Light, and right now, even as we are considering the Immortal Truth ~ the transition in consciousness is taking place, attaining fourth dimensional experience. Your very genes are changing.

All undergoes transformation at the very DNA level, when your mind and heart is stayed on God and utmost Principles of being.

When I speak of transformation, I am talking about you just as you are now, with the great potential already in you ~ only now moving into a greater level of consciousness, performing the consciousness makeover. So you don't even need to start thinking about what form you will be in, as you continue to make changes, for at the root of all the physical is the Divine Pattern of Light, and just know that you are not going to let go of your physical forms 'til you are right and ready, 'til you have accomplished all you want on this plane and throughout the many mansions of existence, 'til your sojourn is complete and you want to be just a dot of light somewhere in the heart of the Universe.

Alright now, if I view my body as it is in the Great Reality, in God's reality, a perfect Divine Idea of harmony and perfection; if I view my body as it is in God... in its pure perfected Divine state ~ I see that it can be only one thing, the reflection, the evidence of pure

Spirit, of Light and Love, of all that Spirit is ...Divine Order of symmetry, beauty, harmony made manifest, condensed into form.

Body is the temple of Divine Life. It is the reflection of Spirit, the microcosm in the macrocosm, reflective of all Divine Powers and Grace, with all organs and parts, every tissue, atom and cell meant to move in perfect, seamless, harmonious function.

During deep meditative periods, I will sometimes say: "God help me just be a reflector of that awesome glory which you are", and boy do I always feel good on those days, when I take time to ask, to stretch consciousness and tap the glory of the Divine Pattern.

Realize the state of the physical is the tangible evidence of the level of one's Spirit, and what you are knowing to be true.

So, if I am dying and leaving my body in a heap, century after century and time after time, who is responsible for this? God? Is my body responsible, or is it something other, operating on the unseen side of life?

Yes, it is myself, and the sum total of all most deeply held thoughts and beliefs, in fact.

Always know, "I am responsible", meaning "I as consciousness, I am responsible for the fate of my body."

The great Immortal Avatar, Babaji, so revered in the East, embodies this Divine Principle of Immortal Life in his physical form, this principle of everlasting life through the eternal maintenance of every aspect at the height of perfection of the Divine Light form, through perfect maintenance of his body and of his molecular, etheric structure, ever renewing it by the pure force of Light and Love. Realize this is our renewing power and capacity too, and this is how we can become the Light body that we are. Babaji understood, of course, that to get to the high place of eternal maintenance of his physical form and to do what he is charged to do, he had to be cognizant that he was in-charge and he was responsible for the fate of his physical instrument. Strive to attain that Highest State of Consciousness, fully cognizant of all the Divine elements present within, that you maintain your body ever in harmony with all that is.

No matter what appears to be going on, always know you are empowered to maintain the body indefinitely, self-renewing at every moment, once unified with the Perfect Principles and Patterns of God within you, once relying on this immense power to bring all things right, in ways even un-thought of. From the very moment of any issue appearing, declare the full healing Presence there.

Know there is that within you that just knows how to heal and the risen consciousness is perfectly equipped to maintain the body indefinitely.

Within you is a Divine Intelligence that cannot be bound. It knows how to heal, for example, a cut in your hand automatically. It knows how to maintain and regenerate itself, this supreme intelligence within your body, within your mind, within your very soul. This power would regenerate all, if only we knew that it would, and would call upon it in every time of necessity and need.

But consciousness must realize it, must realize that this potential is resident within and always taking place, and then through the realization and through right thought and application, through alignment with the Divine within, body will automatically respond by commencing the healing activity that it already knows how to do. It is always the consciousness in these great avatars, and in the Christ that was in total charge of the body and understood right maintenance.

Babaji is living proof, as he sustains his Immortal form in perfection. How great the Love of the perfected soul of Yogananda must have been, so one with all that his body did not suffer decay. How beautiful the resurrected Christ, as the perfect stream of raised consciousness holds his physical form in perfection, and there are many other profound examples of the perfumed and exalted saints, whose bodies never suffered corruption, even after so-called death.

A guru asked to be buried in the ground for two weeks, and came up fine to prove the point that "Look, it is all consciousness."

80

He lived on the elixir of the Divine Breath, even when air underground was not present.

Through the resurrection and following ascension of his physical form, beloved Jesus, Light of the World, showed the Truth of the Immortality and Eternality of the Divine Soul in form. On the mountain of Transfiguration, in an instant he revealed his true form to his beloved disciples...a radiant scintillating body of glowing Light. Now, when he made his ascension, he didn't leave the planet, nor did he go away somewhere or fly off into the sky. As you accelerate your level of knowing, your body molecules ... since they are the perfection of Divine Light, accelerate at the atomic level.

Once, I was driving down the road enjoying all the activity on the West Side Highway and suddenly had an illumination.

I wondered to myself, thinking of the incredible motion of the planets and the spheres, "How fast am I really traveling?" And, suddenly it became so clear, "The speed of light." And so it is that we are always traveling the speed of light, yet seemingly held in place and at lesser speeds by the force of gravity. The mileage may be different on our speedometer, but the fact is we are always traveling at the glorious speed of light.

Now, whenever I am in my car, I like to remind myself: "I am really always traveling at the speed of light."

81

Yet, in the accelerated state of motion, when perception of gravity seems to disappear -~ suddenly all things change, and one's sense of speed and time accelerates too. If someone is zooming by you, somebody running a million miles an hour... You are only going to see a flash of light, you are not going to see them in great detail, although if you slowed the motion down, you would see that it was a person just like you or me.

And, so it is that all is that all is Light in motion...at greater or lesser degrees.

The acceleration which happens through right thinking, and through Highest Spiritual Knowing moves upon and refines your atomic structure and you are automatically then vibrating at a Higher Level. And that is what happened with Jesus, when he went to his Father's House, becoming one with his Higher Perfect Self, one with God. The body was wholly included in that. He didn't leave it in a heap, did he?

As far as I know, it hasn't been found anywhere, so this is the success, the sublime merging into the greater Light of being... and again, really realize that we should think practically about this, not having ideas of ourselves floating about in astral space, lost somewhere, but ground yourself in the knowing that this mighty acceleration is an actual process that is happening within you right now, as you consider Truth...and of course, as you keep working within yourself, aren't you becoming better and feeling better all the time? So you are in fact accelerating right now, every time you have a constructive, spiritual thought. It is nothing different.

By contemplating the Great Reality and by just concentration on it, one is already becoming lighter and lighter, more and more radiant, joyous and free. How wonderful to know we are one with that which can never bound or limited in any way.

Now we are assured that at the Highest Level body is sustained by the pure force of love, breath and light, and we must stop planning to live to die, yet live in the consciousness of blessing Eternity. Most persons live to die, fearful of the inevitable time when this will occur. Most believe that somehow this is a divine dictum, a fate au complete, that is natural and right and so live from day one with in mind to die. No wonder the lifespan at one time apparently so very long, has so significantly shrunk. No wonder now, most have relegated themselves to live around 80 years and some longer. Yet, on the current upswing of consciousness, life spans are gradually improving and extending, as each realizes how much power of longevity they truly possess.

Methuselah knew something, living 969 years, and so too did many of his time enjoy extensive life spans far beyond the ken of modern man, and this comparison is so illuminating and re-invigorating to contemplate as regards the possibilities for one's own life. What did they do or know that was so different, do you suppose? Thus, if we want the Greater Gifts of greater, healthier life spans, not to mention gaining the Pearl of Great Price, consciousness of our *Oneness with the Divine*, we must start planning, you and I ~ right here and now ~ to do better, since we have the great impulse to advance into Higher Levels and be all that we can be, so much more.

The spirit of Divine Evolution compels us further, desiring this new cognition now for our great benefit. We have done a lot of perfecting, so there is no reason why we can't start thinking in terms of this, alright.

Rejoice in who and what you are one with, stop living to die, stop viewing death as inevitable and natural like you were taught. It is not natural in Spirit. Spirit cannot die, nor can anything that is Spirit. Stop seeing yourself as helpless victims and take on a new dimension and awareness, realizing that you can indeed go on forever with right consciousness and right maintenance of the life force as body, and if you choose.

Then, the Infinite skies of Being have no limit for you.

Right maintenance and Highest Understanding is a topmost goal to achieve, learning to rely upon the Infinite Power within for all our healing needs, and coming to this Highest State of Unity is the fulfillment of the great Divine Idea, established by Christ.

Christ came as a wakeup call, to wake up all to the Truth of lustrous and Immortal existence. Caught in a web of materialism, the people were shutting out the spiritual sun, too far away, so he came as a wakeup call to the slumbering masses. In so doing, he changed the world. This is the Divine Idea for each and every one of us...and obviously helpless careening towards death, planning one's whole life around this time when death is going to take place is not the Divine Idea, or what our Heavenly Father/Mother has in mind. So we must continuously ask of ourselves; "What do we want to perpetuate? What Truth do we want to keep creating, perpetuate through our beingness, through our individuality?" Each one of us.

Do you want to attain the perfection of the Christ mind, in living, being and knowing? The perfection of the beloved Christ? What could be greater? What could be greater than this highest aspiration to have all power to bless and raise your life and all lives around you?

Jesus said we will do greater, though most are still struggling to get to that summit point... just to get to his level, but, never forget he said; "You will do greater." So this must be the first work, the realization of only life as power, and learning how to sustain at optimum levels through the Divine Light force that we are. "Ye shall never die, yet shall live forever. Those that believe in me (the Truth) shall not perish." Indeed, God is great. Know: "The Great 'I Am' manifest all that is, as the great perfection of itself, an

85

individual center of Divine Operation." Imagine, you are an individual magnetic center of Divine Operation and this was exemplified through Christ. The potential pattern is already been written within. It has been coded within you, on your DNA. Your Divine DNA structure knows that code but it won't come out until you recognize it, and consciously activate.

Your future in God is already written within you, already encoded by First Cause which brought you into being. Where is it coded? On the Higher Self of your being and mine, the topmost level of your being, the soul behind the soul, the Higher Self, the radiant pattern within. Yet what we have done with this marvelous potential? Through our less than perfect thinking, we have covered over the perfect pattern, with all our negative memories, and all the divergent belief systems, forming a dark cloud. A steely grid has been laid over the perfect pattern and has guised it, obscuring the perfection from us, but what is happening now is the reverse effect. With our humble self-exploration, our willingness to explore the greater spiritual dimensions of ourselves, we are untangling this overlay that has been stopping the light from pouring out, really from our cells, from the very cellular level of ourselves.

The greatest of scientists who have adorned the human plane are forever discovering "that which is" already. There is never anything new to God, and thus even the most exceptional never discovered something new, they just discovered its wonderful existence, like electricity. The potential already existed. Even the most evolved scientist can only reflect to us the discovery of "what is", and how great and Divine, that new findings are happening all the time, revealing the unlimited potential just waiting for our beneficent use. And so it is for mankind, as he/she discovers the Highest Spiritual Principles of Divine and Immortal Life.

Now what is going to happen with all those bacteria organisms with you in the room, when you are saying there is only God, only perfect life? Doctors will be declaring ~ "All my patients are well in Truth, just suffering from a case of mistaken identity." Believe me, the consciousness of any doctor or physician will count, as to providing the most rapid healing of those who come to them for assistance. Scientific studies have recently found out that the heart can go on forever, the actual physical heart. This is in fact revealing the *Spiritual Idea*, the underlying Divine Prototype of the physical heart, meant to be an eternal instrument of Divine Love. Heart can go on forever providing we are not dumping on it all the time, giving it a bad time, and if it is rightly handled. So, how interesting this is? This means that my heart and yours is the greatest Valentine of Eternity, pulsating with the elixir of the never-ending beneficent rhythm of life as us.

The point at which God's love and light flows, the individualization of the cosmic and all-inclusive heart. Each one of us are an individual point where God's love and light can flow and renew, provided we don't get stuck in bitterness, hanging on to hard experiences, holding our experiences in our heart. The heart is the ultimate alchemist, transforming all to Love, changing a poisonous thought or so called "venous" substance, or poisonous substance into the new, clean flow ~ of Love's nurturing elixir. Heart is an alchemical point in the body, a transformational point. That is why we say Love is the refining factor. Love, love, replace whatever negative experience or feeling with Highest Love, and your body will not hold onto poisons of any kind. Imagine, the heart, scientists say now, can go on forever. Well, here we have evidence again of Infinite Eternal life, right where we are…always ours for the claiming, lest we fill our God-hearts with constricting, depressing thoughts and feelings.

Our hearts are constructed to be a perfect instrument of God, a place for Divine Intelligence and Divine Love to flow through, and so is that each and every single organ is a Divine Idea made manifest. The circulatory system represents the great circulation of the cosmos, unobstructed and flowing free. We are a microcosm of the macrocosm and it will be that way for us, when we choose for it to be what it can be, right at the moment of recognition of the underlying spiritual meaning. What is an organ? It is a Divine idea and focusing on this reality is a great healing tool. Let us say somebody has problems with lungs, and on the spiritual plane, we know our lungs represent the inflow and outflow of perfect breath. Lungs purify. Thus it is that my lungs are an idea of God-in-action, perfect. Lungs are streaming that Divine air throughout, enlivening our entire body systems. Claim ~ "The air, indeed the very vital breath of God, streams through my lungs." So, you see how it is that acknowledging the underlying *Spiritual Purpose and Prototype* is a very powerful healing tool that strikes right through to the essential core of the problem. Never mind getting all tied up in asking how did my lungs get this way or that? Take the cure by realizing what they are in God, as a Divine Pattern, and give thanks they are being now that, in the most vitalizing words and in endless gratitude to the Most High that all healing, regeneration, and transformation that needs to take place is now taking place in every way.

Scientists now know this other fact that our thoughts and deepest beliefs get recorded on ourselves, our cells, and behind our cellular structure is the very DNA pattern, the structure which sets the direction of the physical form. Every cell of our being is composed of Living, responsive Intelligence. Everything is mind in form, knowing its perfect function in God and knowing what to do, the embodiment and manifestation of Divine Intelligence in sustaining action and so, when we send in anything other than the Divine Thought of recognition, our cells get the message and conform to our thought, and for a time they play out that lesser pattern. Yet, our original pattern never did and still does not contain death. It is just an illusion. It doesn't contain tendencies towards aging or any of these things. A Great saint said, if a year later in time, I am not looking better and doing better than I was a year before, then something is wrong with me. Something is wrong with my consciousness.

One of my great teachers encouraged to often say to yourself, "I shall maintain this body in perfection, so long as I have need of it"…at the perfect point of maturity that you desire.

So, regarding death, dying, aging and all these limited notions, no, we don't need to have them, we don't need to buy in and why should we. It's not fun. Rather, breathe in the awareness of your eternal sublime life in our Father's House, the true heavenly Garden of Eden, Paradise Found within ~ the perfection of spirit, symbolized by the body physical, where all is Divine, our Father's house where all Divine Activity takes place, Heaven on Earth.

Each can choose to live at the summit level of awareness and in so doing, will immediately begin to manifest the great difference of your enlightened thought. Realize this ~ what we think is immediately physicalized. Spirit is in constant creative action…moving from thought to thing, from inner vision to the outer plane. You cannot have a thought without a follow-up in form, evidence showing up in your manifest world. Your thoughts, silent or out loud, known or unknown move on unseen levels and immediately begin to manifest on the material plane. That which we know to be true is instantaneously physicalized according to the depth of our belief about it. This is the Law of our Being… and understand your freedom in this. Ask yourself, "What do you want to be physicalizing, manifesting? God, Truth, greatness? Perfect health, beauty, peace, well-being?"

Know there is that in you that can...the very essence of the Divine.

If you seek to manifest the perfection of a certain condition, only give thanks to the Most High in you that it is so, and envision yourself already there, vital, flowing and happy, as you would want to be. Keep your eye on the goal, and not on what is transpiring around you. Your very constructive projections and fulfilling expectations will join the action, fortifying and accelerating the arrival of your desired state of wholeness, peace and fulfillment.

As you conceive it and most deeply accept within, so it shall be. Let nothing prevent you from dwelling always in the desirable Divine Outcome.

Once you have freed yourself from any and all ideas of separation from the Most High in you, your Faith and knowledge of the Supreme Power with which you are ever-one will bring a joy beyond knowing. Only the individual can make the greater choice. No one will do it for us. Yet, once you have crossed the invisible dividing line, the barrier standing between yourself and a limitless world of good and freed yourself through your conscious and heartfelt endeavors to understand the Truth, understand God, you are well on your way to a universe of wholeness, peace, fulfillment, and joy beyond anything you have ever conceived…the world of limitless First Cause.

Why try to understand problems? Rather, strive to understand God, understand the Principles of Divine Solution, ever existing simultaneously alongside any and all problems you face.

Once you have freed yourself from buying into the negative conditioning of the collective mind, the force of that mind that ever guises the Light within, you can rise free. This mind is always telling you untruth, so much so that unless you maintain vigilance, it is hard to keep your head straight. Rather live the best life that you can, always being the Best of you, always relating to the Divine Presence and Power in you. It is only buying into negative conditioning that has brought the glory of the Divine Human down.

Yet, by the power of your free will… once you have gotten free enough, you may start to raise up and now embrace the Truth, laying awareness of the vital, supporting substance into the depths of consciousness anew ~ lifting yourself and all around, as you apply the new information on the very cells of your being.

Divine information brings greater life, is always constructive and empowering.

Know: "I am the totality of Light and I am Love", "I am the perfect, ever-renewing health of my Divine Father/Mother, eternally moving throughout the many mansions of splendor (Father/Mother's universe)."

Through steady, conscious effort, and continuously reminding one's self of the glorious Truth that "I and the Father are One" ~ the individual can now replace old limited thoughts and beliefs with life-giving ideas, now imprinting on the deepest levels of subconscious mind what he or she chooses to have there. No more a victim of limitation, continuously choose the Highest and Best patterns of thinking as your new and glorious foundation of being. Know as you love and embody the Highest Truth, this Higher State of being is imprinted on your Divine DNA Pattern.

The structure of the collective mind is changing already. For people's collective thought about themselves is evolving… yet, it is ever so that individuals, pioneering in consciousness, always are striking out first. The crowds will come when you have made it. They get the discovery after you and by your stellar example, but, for yourself, dare to be a leader, a true pioneer, revealing to all the glorious Truth of the limitless Spiritual Nature of Humankind.

Be the living example of this information, so that others can be enlightened through you…and for the sake of the ones who are not in a place, where they can take the first step of themselves.

As long as we say, "Gee…I wish God would come along and help me, and free me and I wish someone else would do it", the liberty you want to achieve not going to happen. How many times have you said, "I just wish that situation would just free me and then you have suddenly the wakeup call that: "Oh my God, I have to free it. I have to free it, myself. And then, I can move on". No one is going to do it for you, unless you have been faithfully working well enough and then of course you will have many friends of High Consciousness to help you, to assist you further and further.

Only faithfully do your right inner work, continuously aligning with Highest Principle and Law, and then the assist, all the help you could ever want shows up. When you are in earnest, humble and loving condition regarding any noble effort, whatever you need just shows up. It is no different for any matter of concern whatsoever. All forces of the universe are attracted to the humble, earnest heart. Each one must perform the transformation on their own. Start by recording ultimate Divine Ideas of limitless Truth on your cells, recording the right information when you mediate on the nature of being. Record your realizations on your DNA pattern and say to yourselves; "My very structure is changing now to exemplify God, the true Divine life that I am…to reflect God."

Your recognition of Divine Truth makes it so for you, and builds the glowing atom of Truth right into your DNA, your actual genes.

It is the most major and rewarding task for anyone to aspire to, one that each one of us must evolve, both individually and collectively, embracing that stellar realization of the pure Divine Life that we are... if we want to raise to another, more heavenly level of existence right here on earth. All potential for unbounded good is contained in the inclusion of God's life as your own.

And what do we do with the rest, the residue of past thinking, all the stuff that has bogged us down?

Burn out all the rest with the fire of Divine and illumined knowing. Burn it out of your being. All negative thought and expectation form a smog on your being, a dark cloud. Simply burn it out. Daily see the sunrise of the light of God sweeping through every atom, tissue and cell of your being and all. See untruth dissolving and being burned out of your entire mental system, all those thoughts and ideas and attitudes and every idea, negative thought and emotion that has kept you bogged down. Sweep it all up and burn it out with the fire of luminous, lustrous Truth...the Truth that shall set you free.

You don't even have to get into it. Like the great Fritz Pearls said, you don't have to inspect your garbage, just dump it, and then fill your heart and mind with the radiant, nurturing waters of Divine Mind, consciously exchange the lesser and matter-bound for the Greater Truth, that knows no limit of possible good for you.

95

The Light of God is right there within the center of your Heart and Soul, so burn all dross out by the Light within you. Be aware and daily strive to clean up your total thought atmosphere, by aligning all with Divine Love and Light. Be not a walking, talking smog or cloud. Everybody has an atmosphere. Haven't you been around somebody that is into negation and negativity? Don't you feel like: "Oh, they are putting this heavy stuff on me, and all around. "Oh! A black fog has come!" A feeling of density surrounds us, when in contact with such persons. The negativity projected is so dense and heavy, because it is so apart from the Light of Spiritual Being, and this is the destructive force called death.

This is what careens you toward death, the heaviness of negative thought. Light catapults you toward ever-expanding life.

At this stage of ascension we are purifying and there is the cleaning out our total thought atmospheres. Now, you know you have an atmosphere because you can feel it when you are around a person who is heavy and you know how you feel when you are around a Divine and enlightened being. These are two entirely different matters. Each one of us can use that cosmic energy to flow the Light throughout all, clean it up, rising above.

Determine to rise above boring statistics and endless repetition and establish the Kingdom of Heaven, which is Truth, God's Kingdom on earth, meaning here... in the world of form, in the material plane and throughout our mental, physical, emotional systems.

Right here and now is the place for ascension, not somewhere else, not sometime else, yet right here. Now, there is one other factor to consider, before we once again center in the Heaven of Truth within, through meditation. If you choose to go all the way ~ it is not enough to say; "It's okay." "Well, I'm doing well spiritually, but really, that has nothing to do with my body." Realize, it doesn't work that way, for all is one.

You want to come to the place where there is no division in your thinking whatsoever, where you know that you know: "There is only thing and that is Spirit." Every aspect of body, mind and spirit is interconnected. There is not this and that, existing in various states of separation. The quality of one's thoughts stir the feeling life in negative or constructive expectation and vision. The quality of one's thought life can raise an organ into healed perfection or cause it to droop in utter sadness. Your very bloodstream is energized by Divine Light.

Realize that if your spirit and intelligence is truly involved in the right manner and with the sense of totality, so too your heightened state automatically shows up in your body. People will be amazed, as your whole appearance changes....on a good day in your mental household. When you are centered in constructive thinking and peaceful expectation of only good, all your body cells shine with Divine Life.

Strive to incorporate Divine Love all the way, and your body will reflect the radiant life of God-in-you. Don't let it be enough to love just sometimes. Of course establishing love with all those you hold near and dear and those you hold great attraction for is wonderful, but, to truly don the cloak of the Divine Self, you also want to come to the place where you truly have love for all. Remember, you are a Divine generator of this sublime and life-giving force, wherever you are.

And, in your thoughts and aspirations towards complete well-being know that you must now include body, your heavenly home and temple here, and in all of your knowing, no longer saying body is something else, and not a part of the Divine.

If not, you'll be dumping it again in a pile again for someone else to pick up. Ask yourself, does spirit die? Are you 100% sure of this? Is there anything that is not spirit? Ask yourself, if you 100% believe all is Spiritual in Essence, and if that is the case, why are you dying your body? Such a mind-set that leads to death and destruction doesn't work anymore, once the greater horizon of Truth has come into view. Learn to constantly regenerate your body, by your thought of your Unity with the Perfect Body of God. Learn to maintain your body in the most desired state of perfection for you.

Do as much as you can, while on the material plane, for even those rest periods, shuffling off the mortal coil for a while, still won't add to your knowing, unless you have used your life experience to the best possible level of applied Truth.

That means, right in the midst of trying conditions, giving thanks for the perfection to emerge. Wherever you have gained Truth, it now is with you always.

Realize that all practices that lead you to embrace Higher Truth and experience greater well-being are wonderful, yet the key difference with the Higher Consciousness approach and understanding the Science of Mind ~ is that we work to transform everything in consciousness first, because therein is the root of every issue, resting in the beliefs held most deeply in mind. While you enjoy all the many methods that exist to help you on the path, never forget the primary power of your consciousness. Highest consciousness mixed with tools of holistic understanding is a combination that can't be beat, whether in the form of acupuncture, acupressure, or chiropractic adjustment, for all are working with alignment and are rooted in the Divine Principle of balance.

Yet, realize that if you feel limited to physical solutions only, to any physical means for your wellness, you haven't got the whole thing, you just haven't got it yet, for you are depending on something outside your very own Light body within.

So, I'm not saying don't do those things you enjoy. By all means, you must do them until you come to a place where you can realize that God is all and then you will say, well, there is nothing to be healed and not in a flippant way, but realizing that there was nothing wrong to begin with, it was just a wrong idea about it. The very cell that you once called cancerous then becomes well ~ and shows itself to you as the light of God that it is, in the instant that you have realized there is no cancer. It is not a reality. It is an idea.

If you need medicine, do take it, declaring all the Presence and Power of God acting through that particular treatment....reminding yourself about the placebo effect, where persons have gotten perfectly well by taking prescribed pills and other forms of medicine, which in fact were composed of just plain water and gotten well, thinking it was filled with curative substance, thinking it was something else.

It matters not what path we take, it matters our consciousness about it. Our efforts are always successful, where we declare the whole Presence and Power of God operating through all methods undertaken, but know behind all is that Pure Presence that we are believing in, doing the work.

By the Law of Belief, a thing will work if we believe it does, yet, on the other hand and quite to the contrary if we bottom-line believe that nothing can cure us, then nothing will. Therefore, bless every path you are guided to take in any healing, knowing the Creator is smiling behind and the treatment you have chosen is doing its perfect work, that all things are working together for good.

.

Ultimately, we will come to the supreme understanding that body can heal itself.

Meantime, if you believe that it can, so it does. If you believe any treatment is working, so it does.

The thing itself doesn't have anything in it except God. It is nothing other than God. The thing of itself doesn't have anything special about it. It is the consciousness behind it. So, we say penicillin is the cure, but when the discovery of this miracle cure came about, we were willing to find a cure and we dubbed penicillin the cure, but really it was our collective acceptance in consciousness.

All of these Truths become more and more evident to you as you concentrate upon the true and limitless life of God that you are, understand the power of consciousness and beliefs, and begin to utilize The Divine and Incomprehensible healing principles that exist for each and all.

Another thing to know in healing is that an experience can only exist as long as you maintain it by giving it your consciousness attention, and I have seen every kind of life-threatening condition disappear and transform to perfect health, the instant a person has realized the underlying meaning of why an issue had appeared, and is willing to let it go. When the purpose is fulfilled, and if your consciousness is not holding on to the condition, it will dissolve. It takes your consciousness to hold a thing in temporary form.

Anything that helps us is good and we really believe this because all methods are really God-in-action, and it all can serve us very well, but we must realize that ultimately there was never any power to that malady to begin with, yet, for whatever our reasons, we made it a fact for ourselves ~.giving it a form for a while.

Now, for example, if a person who has manifested an unwanted condition realizes that he or she manifested that condition to get the attention of someone ~ they can begin to get the attention in other, more fruitful ways.

Basic psychology will tell you that people sometimes get illnesses, because on a subconscious level, it is the only way they think they can gain the attention so desperately wanted. Thus, if the person can realize the underlying benefit they are seeking ~ find a way to constructively get the attention sought through another way, they can simply let that go. They no longer have to manifest the troubling condition. and they can still get what they want in perfect freedom, joy and peace...with no toll on body, mind or Spirit, no double-edged sword.

One of the fastest treatments to accelerate the healing action is to declare: "Right where that issue is, whatever it is, (let's forget about labeling) "is the whole totality of God". This is a very powerful statement that will serve to stimulate the Divine Healing Powers. Another very powerful mantra is; "Perfect God, Perfect Man, Perfect Being".

"Perfect God, perfect man, perfect woman, perfect being." We know that evolution for the better in all our concerns will show up and our physical forms will become more refined, as we progress further and further in our understanding of our Immortal Self. We know that Spirit doesn't die, and mankind's destiny is simply unlimited as to how much of the Divine Self can be realized.

Let us take a moment now to dwell upon the limitless Truth and gain empowerment about any situation of prime concern to you. The following exercises will help you to see what it is that you need to release, if you desire to follow in the footsteps of the Great Ones.

CHOOSE THE HIGHER OPTION

Take a deep breath, getting as quiet as you can, and once you feel calm and centered, look within, being as honest as you can, as you contemplate the following question. Remember the purpose is not to criticize ourselves, but to bring up that all that stuff that has been hindering, that it may be transformed.

We want to clean out our atmosphere…so that it is radiating with the Life of God, that our blood becomes the Blood of Light, that wherever we are, our inner life gives off the beneficent aroma of the most magnificent rose.

Look from the High Place at all areas of your life, and just write down right now where you still feel that there are certain special areas that you feel do not apply to the laws of Eternal Spirit, that somehow these special issues exist under some type of other government than Divine Love and Law, and just be honest… or even if you feel insecure about something, just write it down.

Note the key areas where you are struggling with this concern, and where you are still experiencing difficulty ~ any key areas where you are still experiencing victim consciousness in any aspect of your expression of your pure God life force, always totally successful and always victorious. Note any area where your expectations don't measure up to the glory of God-in-you.

Be sure and mark down areas where you feel that these situations somehow are special cases and don't apply to the laws of Eternal Spirit, i.e. they can never be cured.

Note any areas of helplessness, too, and after you've done that, I'd like you to bring up any fears that you may have about Eternal Life or objections, any areas of helplessness where you still feel at the mercy of outer forces, where you feel you have no choice, suffering under the feeling of victimhood. Know that whatever surfaces will be the right thing that you are ready to address and heal right now, including any fears or misgivings about Eternal Life. You are now ready to heal this situation in Perfect Truth.

Realize that every thought, feeling or belief that constricts even a little constricts the whole thing, your entire world of experience and manifestation. And, for the purposes of this exercise, and specifically regarding fear of the unknown and the future, I would like you to address a separate portion of your self-questioning to the idea of living forever. I'd like you to see if there are any fears in there, because by the Law, what we fear or have objections to of any sort, we will resist. Once you have written down and identified your chief areas of concern, ask yourself what is your Higher Divine Option in this matter.

What can you know, claim and assert for yourself that is more commensurate with your Divine Self?

In all instances, you have the Higher Option, and the capacity to choose to change your negative expectation to the Spiritual Opposite of Victory, Love, Perfect Healing, Perfect Manifestation and Joy. Instead of fear, you can practice the Faith that knows no bounds, instead of succumbing to situations truly not appropriate for you, know there is always a perfect God-way to extricate yourself from such circumstances, and to attract the very best instead. If you rely upon the Perfect Presence of Spirit in all matters ~ you will come up victorious, always in the most harmonious way.

Although it takes spiritual stamina and firm commitment to apply Faith, for instance, in the midst of fear...consider the advantages and disadvantages for you ~ which is greater, being brave and trying on the new thing right in the midst, or just going along in the same old way.

Which can produce the greater benefit for you?

Once a woman, a teacher, confronted a major dilemna, in that she had received a notice for jury duty, and yet, her spiritual conscience was completely centered in the principle of "Thou shalt not judge." She was extremely uncomfortable, not knowing how to address. She believed in being a "responsible" citizen, yet everything about this went against her mission as a healing person.

As we talked, I encouraged her to write up her true reasons, write a note asking to be excused from serving, since her heartfelt objection was not to dump responsibility, yet genuinely arose from conflict with her deeply held sense of purpose, not to mention her students would be bereft of her presence for an indeterminable amount of time. Truly expressing herself from her heartfelt center would always bring the best result.

In this time of awakening, each must live their purpose. Each must do what feels right for us to do, that feels harmonious with our individual purpose and spirit. And, in the case where imposed obligations arise, she would need to let go off any type of ideas of false obligations. These are collective mind ideas, but she was not obligated to go along, and needed to release the idea that she was not being a good citizen in conventional terms.

If it was not in the movement of her spirit to put herself in charge of someone's life, in that way, then she should definitely not perform the service.

Rather, by all means she needed to communicate her heartfelt position, because that is what is required. And then, better yet, daily take a moment to pray for the perfection of the case in her mind's eye, and for the perfect solution to come about for everyone concerned. Just treat for God's perfection to manifest in the case. I then encouraged her to free herself from any feeling of guilt, and so she proceeded to honestly notify them of her position, and she was immediately granted permission in perfect understanding and grace, and was excused.

Indeed she exercised her Higher Option, remaining faithful to herself, and served the public good in her own way, knowing there were certainly plenty of persons who would like to be in there. They did not need her, in that way. This took courage for her to do, to take a stand for her true beliefs, thereby overcoming not only her own fear and guilt, but the expectation of not being heard. Certainly, all supported her in Grace, and she learned a new thing.

So often, we feel if we don't go along with the show and do what everybody else is doing, then we might be doing something wrong, and we'll be rejected, and so we continue to live out collective programming, tradition ~ afraid to step out of the group thinking mode on our own, standing by the God-Self.

A very different example of collective programming would be that at a certain point, your hair has to turn grey. You wouldn't be right if you didn't turn your hair gray, you wouldn't be a right person. How does one counter such notions?

In order to let the color flow again, realize if one has a belief my hair must turn, and that it is right and proper for one's hair to turn to such and such color at such and such age, we have immediately stymied the color producing agents. My mother's hair, by the way doesn't have any grey hairs ~ and she is in her late 90's. She is living proof of that consciousness that knows no bounds. Realize it is the very consciousness of a person that then flows the blood, stimulates the Immortal glands, and supplies all the sustaining action, providing all the necessary ingredients to produce the texture and constant regeneration of color. So, if you find yourself turning grey, just forgive yourself for thinking you had to turn grey, and then start giving thanks that your circulation is completely whole and that your hair is coming out the color, which seems right for you. People have re-grown their own hair. Right thought stimulates expansion of brain cells, and manufacture of perfect growth substance.

Your destiny in all things is up to you. Just realize that collective programming runs very deep and if left unmonitored, we play it out just like we are a record. Someone just put the needle on us and we'll play the song we are used to singing, until we get individualized. When we get individualized and we understand that we are working with a power that is Infinite beyond imagining, the horizons open wide, and we know we can never be stuck in any condition at all, unless we believe that we can.

There is nothing that this Power cannot do. When we understand that, we can step away from the collective mind, from hapless traditions that bind and limit, and we can make our glowing statements, and be the living and transcendent proof.

And we must use our mighty gift of will in this way…to always place our Faith in the Greater. A very great yogi told me once a very great secret. He said, "No compromise." He said, once you start compromising, you can never get what you want. So when in lackluster thinking, you are teaching yourself how to never to be able to get what you want and what is compromise? Compromise is buying in to something other, lesser than the pure idea.

Thus, we must stick with our goals until we get there knowing a whole universe backs us up in every noble pursuit.

We want to stop engaging in this destructive habit. Once you compromise with Truth, you are lowering your will, your Divine faculty and gift of will and pretty soon, it doesn't have any energy and you die. This is a major factor in the trajectory we will set. God gave us the precious gift of will. Will is the dynamic creative force. If we are not using our Divine Will aright ~ to sustain and stand-by our true identities in God, we cannot truly achieve the goals we treasure. We cannot have freedom to truly use our will until we become free of collective mind, pulls and pushes, and until we become our own authority and stop buying in to every other authority ~ that means what the "they say", and " it's always been this way." And the "no one else has done it." Know that what keeps somebody going, is the Divine Fire of Will… your conscious choice and decision to lengthen your life to whatever time you determine, and whatever state, level and quality of being you desire.

Through the constructive forces of faithful will and determination, we can and do bring all right.

I am not talking about the use of your will to force matters through. I am talking about the decision to align with the Highest and the Best in you. Such Highest use of your Divine Will 'will' flow, what you need to you, opening the secret doors.

But if you just give up and say whatever life wants to throw at me, o.k., and poor helpless me, you are going to get the results of whatever the popular opinion is within your world of associations, and that you are buying into. So either you are going to establish your destiny for yourself, because it is your choice, it is your will, or you will allow the will of others to dominate your life. And this great yogi went on to say to me; "With your will and your faith, is there anything you cannot do? With your Divine Soul Powers of Faith and Will, is there anything you cannot do?", and I had to say, "Well, of course, there isn't."

But if one is equivocating, which one is always perfectly free to do, you can see how much weaker the energy for your desired manifestation is. It is easy to see how the whole of humanity has fallen under the slumber of that sleeping will and it is usually not until people get in to metaphysics, when they get inner spiritual consciousness and realize their oneness with God again ~ that they begin to feel the flow of "I can", once again stimulating the heart.

"There is a chance for me now", and that is the will waking up and feeling "I can." Always know that with your will and your faith pointed in fruitful direction, there is nothing that you cannot do.

In certain areas of the world, people live apart from society in small villages and are known to live to a great age, well over one hundred years, and all members of the group do the same.

111

Over time, each new life is copying the benevolent status quo around them, and such a strong standard reinforces the patterns of long life. There are certain ones who are the pioneers. Einstein went ahead and discovered what existed. He was a pioneer. Ford was a pioneer of the auto industry.

Great people go out ahead of the crowd, transcendent of the status quo, and establish that new and wonderful pattern that the crowd can then feel comfortable to copy and that is exactly true.

For some of us, we have to go out there first. And that is what I am saying. Don't wait for the crowd to jump on the band wagon. Know that with your will and your faith, you can do anything that is Divine, including charging up all those cells that are producing the glorious hair, the beautiful skin, but if you say… "I wonder if I can do it", you are not applying the force of your will. There is no power in that. Rather, affirm: "I am deciding to do it, because it is the original Divine Idea", and then meditate on your joyous success morning, noon and night.

If you are not seeing results right away, only know you are as yet living in two thoughts ~ and there is yet conflict to resolve.

Supposing you feel that the only problem is that you don't want to live to one hundred? Ask yourself, why would that be? Clearly, there must be some negative thought compelling.

112

Perhaps you feel you'd rather get a new life and body, than live in pain. Ask yourself, what do you say in your self- talk that is a result of collective thought… is a result of hearsay?

Have you heard that the body will break down and deteriorate, and you will have to live in pain?

Be aware of the negative influence that got in there, as you accepted this unfortunate fate. Ask; "Does the same have to be true for you?" No, it doesn't if your mind and heart is stayed on God and all that is radiant life. Ask yourself: "If you choose to occupy this plane of existence for a greater amount of years, do you have to have any pain whatsoever to qualify?" From the point of view of your Divine Self, can you see now the real Truth?

Can you now declare to yourself who is in charge of how you live?

When you unearth your objections to living as long as you want, you will always find some negative projection at cause.

Here, you have total authority to change the path of your perceived destiny, by centering in the wonderful Truth of your Divine and Eternal Self, and in so doing, and claiming the wonderful pain-free life to be yours, so shall it be. Everything in you will now move to create that scenario you now envision for yourself. In the

113

new knowing of your freedom, change all negative projection to utmost positive, joyful pictures and expectation of your Divine Self, healthy, whole and complete at every point in time.

Aren't you free? Is there really some force on the outside locking you in to some type of repetitive pattern?

Once an individual realized how much he had been compromising, and once discovering the source of the continuous round of nagging issues…he decided to throw all those notions off and be healthy and live better and better each and every day. Nothing stops him now.

Ask yourself what quality of life do you want to live? If you knew that you could create any pattern for your health and well-being, what would that be?

Deeply contemplate the quality of life you would want to experience, regardless of how long you live. What kind of shape do you want to be in?

Of course you would want to maintain the best of health, strength, beauty and vitality. Realize, even as you would speak the words most meaningful to you, the alchemy is already taking place from within, as your subconscious mind responds in kind to the vital picture you are now putting before it.

Once you have arrived at that radiant new picture you truly want for yourself, then make it the Law of your being, not only for right now, but for Eternity. Forget about stopping in time. Establish permanent patterns of exquisite health forever right now. Dwell upon them daily, envisioning yourself in the new and optimum condition, giving thanks that this is so. Why stop at 80, 90, 100, or any determined time frame?

Make perfect health and victory over any weaknesses or illnesses your permanent pattern, always available to you.

In society, everyone says you have to remember what age you are. Yet, in your best moments, don't you feel so timeless, that you can't even remember. Doesn't the matter of age seem so insignificant?

Let it always be this way for you. Declare to yourself one of the most magnificent mantras of Truth ~ "I am ageless, timeless, deathless being," and let others work it out and marvel at your wonderful condition…their state of shock at your confidence in the Truth. What are your qualifications to be eternally healthy and the peak of life? Your Divinity, your Divine Nature, the Light within.

Know: *"I am one with God…. And, so are you!* Know the Truth of lustrous freedom, available to each and to all. Support all in their quest for perfect health, knowing the Divine Power is in all.

115

Start your ascent into perfect health and well-being, in the now. Start now. If someone comes along and says to you, oh, you are X amount of years old, it is too late and such and such a condition is unavoidable. Stand up within, and re-affirm to yourself: "I am not doing that." Watch yourself and what you are automatically accepting as true. Everywhere around lesser ideas are being impressed upon your psyche. You get on the subway, signs will say, "Oh, you're 40 years old, have your eyes been checked yet? Your vision lessens as you get older. Give us a call!" And there you have it. If you accept that internally, you are roped in, and are now in danger of that condition. Realize when you are just buying into somebody else's or society's idea and where you have been just playing it out, someone else's idea for you.

Though we live in time, realize you are ageless, timeless being, and though time exists on earth for the convenience of our sense of order and for the sake of identifying hours and minutes of structured existence, live in a consciousness of your eternal Reality. We abide on planet Earth, thus, we use linear time, so never be afraid to say what age in Earth years you are, but in your heart, live beyond linear time, knowing you are ever Eternal Spirit in the now.

Always be clear and don't label yourself anything at all, for ~ you see, the instant you do it, you set the train in motion for yourself. Look rather to the greatness of Divine Cause in you. Stretch yourself far beyond boundaries of the past.

Look at what you have planned for yourself before you knew that you could create something better, and write it down, then evolve a picture of the Divine You prevailing. Nothing can continue to hurt you if you bring the issue out there, where you can see it, bring it up before your conscious mind. Just notice whatever comes up, and realize you are not bound to that: "I was planning to be in pain, because that is what those around me did and that is what I have seen, and all I have been envisioning." Once you see that, by the power of your Divine Will, you can now say no to that picture, declaring you no longer support that or plan to live by that, yet you plan to unfold the glory of the Divine Self within, filled with never-ending renewing life force and all power to overcome.

This is the power of your Divine Will, to say "No, not a chance, I don't care who has done it for how long, I am not doing this." Use your "I am" Power, your real power within, that is ever one with God. When you make your statements to yourself, try and state only that which is Eternally True, not temporary and passing. It is perfectly okay to notice something going on: "I am having an experience of poor health", for example, but know there is that in you which is greater, and surely you shall overcome by relying on the greater and all-encompassing power of renewal within.

The greater the negative thought, the more you want to affirm and declare the spiritual opposite of wholeness and peace: "I am manifesting the opposite. I am becoming healthier each and every moment that I breathe. As you tell your body and your psyche this blessing information, all will begin to restore, as the subconscious which forms your life experience thrives on the new information given. Every cell of your being will just rejoice.

And then start building the consciousness of that new and vibrant state you have in mind. That means every night before you go to sleep, indeed every moment ~ Give Thanks that you are becoming eternal health that knows no disease or infirmity. Give thanks for what you want, for, by the Law you must give the mind a new pattern to form for you.

Yet, it is not enough to say no to what you don't want to find yourself creating, you also need to define the wonderful new condition you are now setting for yourself, in the place of the old. Now, regarding any other fears, simply ask yourself: "How would I be if I did not have these fears?" And then, begin to give thanks that you are that. This is how you raise yourself scientifically Everything is consciousness and intelligence, and all begins by an idea held in the invisible realms of mind. Thus, be aware and consciously choose what you want to experience and any time you get into a dull frame of mind about it, just notice that, sit down with yourself and commune with your Divine and Perfect Self of God, with your Higher Self. Re-center in your goal and ask, "What is it I was doing again? I seem to be off track." And never say quit. Instead of saying, "if "I make it", rather declare: "I will keep going 'til I make

REVEREND DR. LINDA DE COFF

it." If you get into "ifs", you are never going to full transcend, for you are putting the power outside yourself. Every enlightened person will tell you that all outcomes rest in your power of choice and definite decision. You cannot equivocate or be wishy washy, because you are the only one who is in charge.

Simply monitor your thinking and take out those negatives, which weaken the possibilities of achieving your objective by saying, "No, I see I am thinking that. No. This is not taking place in my life. The law of my life is; "I am establishing permanent habits of success, I am establishing, permanent, perfect health, because of God-in-me. And I will keep going until I have overcome any other tendencies ~ until I am 100% transcendent of the old issues and perfectly joyous and successful." Why? "Because I am the success of God- in- action, and there is no failure is God. There is no failure in Spirit, therefore there shall be none in me."

So you see how we can use our will and our power. Rightly used, the Divine Will is tremendous, tremendous power for good ~ capable of establishing the best that can be in an instant. Now, I know you have experienced the profound power of decision at some time in your life and you know what a great force this will, this decision is. Stay with your vision 'til you get there: "I am succeeding, and I don't care how long it takes. I am not going to get hung up in time. I am going to do my right work, because I know if I do my right work in consciousness, I will experience greater good than I ever conceived of", and meantime... Give Thanks to your Source, which responds to you and streams through you the complete substance of whatever your mind is on, manifesting the tangible experience.

Live in the state of Gratitude continuously: "Thank you, every moment I am feeling healthier. Something great is going on with me." Every moment of the day, and every night before you go to sleep, Give Thanks that you wake up and you are pain-free. You don't have to know where it went. It just went. "Thank-You-In-Advance." You don't have to know where the pain or the problem went, do you? The Divine has ways and means. It got taken away. Let it be taken away. It is so simple.

Regarding objections, realize that if you object to something on any level, known or unknown you will not manifest it. And, if you think the manifestation of your goal will mean that something you don't want will come along with it, there is no way you are going to manifest that.

And so it is very important for your bright future to continuously bring up these old thoughts, that they may be healed.

Try not to wait to get to the point where you are in 100% in pain to begin with, and rather cultivate your Divine Consciousness of the life that you are. Get to the 100% level in manifesting absolute health and you will be helping not only yourself, but all other people around you.

Know your body is a Divine Instrument that can be regenerated constantly. Why should muscles atrophy? Why should your physical household start to fall apart. Can you tell me… does Spirit atrophy? Then why do we do this? Because they told us to, we are just playing it out.

So don't buy into that. Affirm; "I am the perfect mobility of spirit, I am the intelligence of perfect spirit, flowing through me."

When my teacher chose to make its departure at 107, he was intelligent, bright, a great speaker, possessing and living the whole thing, nothing was missing. No missing parts.

Now making your departure is your choice, whenever you choose to do it. How fortunate we are to have the benefit of all these great beings, who have shown us the secrets of transcendence, and through their very own lives, have revealed the great secrets of the Kingdom of Immortal life, the sacred mysteries of how to perpetuate life indefinitely. Think of yourself as Perfect Spirit, and when any idea comes before you ~ Ask: "Is this true in Spirit? True in God?"

Know, "If it is not true in God, it is not true for me, no matter how many years or lifetimes I may have believed it."

Supposing you have learned that you have to work hard all your life to make a living. Counter this with Truth. Does *Perfect Spirit* ever stress or strain? Is there anything hard for Spirit? If it isn't true for Spirit, it is not true for you.

Does the Divine in us ever do anything with moaning and groaning and exorbitant effort? Ask yourself, what is the Divine Pattern of work for Spirit? What is the Highest and best you can conceive of, the ultimate pattern for you of grace, peace and poise, that you would be so exalted in the doing of...and when the answer, the Divine solution, arises in your mind ~ begin to give thanks that this work and this life style is now yours. In all areas of life, we want to activate the Divine Pattern of Peace, Poise, and Eternal Grace.

And, if you would like to know more in depth information about Divine Principle, Patterns and Laws of the Highest Self, be sure and pick up a copy of my book, "Mysticism & Ultimate Divine Healing Processes, the Perfect Principles and Patterns of God!" Here you will find in-depth applications of Highest Healing Power to every department of life...whether physical, mental or emotional well-being, relationships, finances or work.

Ask: Is what you are believing merely a recording of the traditional thought field around you? Are you still playing it out in your life, rather than expressing the glory of the Divine You?

If you are working so hard that there is no enjoyment, for example, think of what exalted conditions you'd want to put in its place, if you knew that you could. Obviously, you don't want the lesser, or to be a slave to any less than fulfilling pattern. Nobody wants that. I mean, you might as well never go to work in that consciousness. As you contemplate and embrace the new God-idea for your richest fulfillment and dwell on that ~ Your work patterns are going to change, to become the embodiment of joyous self-expression, always in a beneficial atmosphere and most appropriate position, for that is what Perfect Spirit wants for you.

Ask yourself, what is the Divine Pattern of work for unlimited Spirit as you? And, as soon as the benevolent picture comes to mind, begin to give thanks that this wonderful work is now yours.

Always move into Gratitude to that unseen force that shapes our lives and that responds to the ideas we give it. The subconscious mind is all one with God, with all the capacity. Your thoughts go deep into this soil of mind, and produce the perfection of results for you. As you have given thanks, so it shall be.

Never worry about the ways and means, for Divine guidance will flow forth, as you dwell on the Divinely Desirable picture for you. See yourself there already in your mind's eye, knowing the Divine is taking care of everything necessary, that all persons, places and things that are a part of your new good are coming together in perfect, harmonious ways and means.

Every ounce of joyous fulfilling existence that you add unto your life, adds energy to your Immortal genes, restoring and revitalizing every atom and cell of your being, removing burden and age.

If others are suffering around you, know they have unconsciously made their negative experiences so…by the nature of their beliefs, the individual has unknowingly made it the Law of his or her being. But, do you have to do the same? These encumbrances never need to belong to you, if you know the Higher Laws and the degree of freedom that you have. If someone has fallen into negative conditions, it becomes temporarily so, but only for that individual. Why do you have to do the same? Why would you? So others can feel good, not because you have to.

Do what you love, identify what is the Divine Thing that you do best and strike out on that and you will have no financial problems.

As long as you are buying into the victim thing and you are not knowing that you can set optimum goals of peace, power and plenty for yourself ~ then you will be subject to the force field around you. That is one level of how negative conditions can appear. When we don't want to do the creative work necessary within ourselves, somebody else has to give us rules and regulations and we end up having to punch their time clock.

Yet, when we know we have a great thing to do, as an individualization of the Divine on this earth and when we start asking the right questions... "What is it about me that is unique? What are my talents?" ~ the right answers come. When we start talking with God, the Creative Force, and asking this Unlimited Source of "All that Is" to illumine a right place for expression of our talents, affirming "I know that you will cover me, you will supply me, get me where you want me to be."...all things good and wonderful appear before us, showing the way.

And, when you are willing to let go of all that comes in between that purity of Divine Relationship and you, such as "they are going to cut me off, if I follow my own inner leadings", "they are going to make me suffer for following my own path", and on and on...you will rise to enjoy the Kingdom the Divine has prepared for you. It takes courage to stand out from the masses, but the rewards are beyond compare.

The old system of connections will try and make you feel fear, if you are not sure of your unique status in God. We are not going to insure you, you won't get the benefits, because you didn't sacrifice your entire timeline ~ earth plane existence to us. In such moments of doubt and fear of doing your own thing, know: "In my Father's house are many mansions", and you will always have what you require, always in right Divine ways,, for nothing can interfere with the force of God in your life and that sustains you, in most perfect and right ways for whatever you need.

Maintaining complete reliance on the Higher in you is the most practical attitude to have...the one that can move the mountains into the sea, open every door, and supply you endless prosperity of income in Infinite Ways and Means. It is not practical for you to spend your life playing out the lesser and dumping yourself and your body in the grave and then starting all over again. It is not practical.

It is practical to know that there is God, your great Divine Resource for all things desirable, healthy and good...to know that you are special and unique and magnificent, you have something great to do, to invest all of your heart and your energy in finding out what that is, and giving it and doing it and the rest shall follow. I guarantee you.

I have lived this story all of my life, and hardly ever worked for anyone in anything, unless by glad choice. It always pays off, always...to follow your true heart, to live in Faith. Yet, ~ it is important to be aware of the terrorism that lurks underneath. This is collective programming; this is the subconscious garbage that is limiting us, killing us in every way. Ask yourself, what have you heard about your particular aspiration? Supposing you decided to go off and do your own thing and trust in God, what does the group mind you are associated with threaten you with? Then, declare the Truth of Infinite and Eternal Support, in perfect right ways.

Can God ever be depressed, financially? Is God out of anything ever? If you are the only person on the earth whose mind is on God and the rest are into the recession, you will be prospering, for according to your transcendent Faith and knowing, God will produce the substance of moneys or anything else you require directly for you, now ~ according to your unswervable Faith. If all doors seem closed to you, all that you need would just manifest directly and of itself from the One Divine Source, sustaining all.

There indeed have been times when I have needed cash and there weren't even any coins in my pocket, and suddenly, when I would look again, I would discover that coins had manifested, where none were only a moment ago. Where did they come from, some hidden pocket? Indeed, they manifested from the very substance of my thought, as I affirmed Infinite Supply. Thus, ask yourself what are the fears that you have about this issue of going off on your own to do your own thing?

Perhaps you fear you might fail? Lots of people do. You don't want to be one of them. Perhaps you anticipate extreme embarrassment, if that were so.

Even so, stand in Faith, and do all you can to manifest the good sought for yourself.

Once the hidden fear is discovered, ask: "What Truth could you possibly now know to replace this fear, a Truth of the Divine and Eternal You?" Now in order to dump this we must realize that one of the main reasons fear arises…and one of the main causes of fear is when we have designated the authority somewhere else than in ourselves.

Then we get to be afraid, and rightfully so, because everyone else is now in charge of our life. In such moments, affirm: "There is only one authority in my life and that is God, the totality of Divine Principle, Presence and Law. I am the Principal of Divine Success that cannot fail. I do not entertain failure, because I am a Divine Being and I always succeed in everything that I do. I do not permit that failure language to come in where God is concerned anymore because there is no failure in God. Therefore there is no failure in me. I am the success of God."

In order to transcend and transform fear into a Faith that knows no opposite, you want to build up spiritual stamina, founded in Truth, thereby extricating yourself. First, realize you are reacting, that the fear has arisen, and then quite consciously tune up your thought to God. Ask yourself; "Is this that I fear a possibility for God?" If it is not a possibility for Perfect Spirit, then it is not for you. Remain in a state of Divine courageousness. You are the one to make your choice of alignment...at every point of concern, affirming: "It is not a possibility for me", and you must be brave enough to say, I don't care what the "they say". Who are these they(s)? And who formulated these statistics, and wherefrom drawn and assessed?

Statistics are the reflection of any particular group mind, and most often of those who have not awakened as yet, nor individualized themselves in God.

The choice is always yours. It is always up to you. What belief system do you want to live out?

When you know you are one with Divine Life and all that it is... your entire world of associations change. Persons find themselves choosing a far better group of friends, selecting personal company even better, as one strives to totally come out of negative, competitive spheres. That is picking and choosing your friends wisely and it is so wonderful to do. In one's free time, the individual should always hang out with right supporting and inspiring, joyous company.

Your free time is yours, and as you are building up your own individuality, right association will bring empowerment and constructive re-enforcement, not only to you, but to all.

129

And I have found this to be a very excellent and healing thing to do. Very often… if I will look at fear in the face, and if I would actually ask the underlying question surrounding the possible negative consequences I might be afraid of, i.e.; "Supposing I did fail? Does that have to stop me?" I will suddenly see that it doesn't. Of course you would never fail when you say that to yourself, but, if this should be your fear, ask, "Supposing I do?" "Supposing what they say is so?" "Is that all right?" At least I will have gone out and given it a shot, and will have learned something to make my next attempt better. By that time you'll probably be long gone and graduated to your next expanded level of unbounded success.

If you can let it be okay if you fail, then you won't set up unconscious forces of resistance and strain, thinking; "I want to, but I'm afraid."

Only those who are unaware would ever dream of not encouraging you.

And, if you are surrounded by jealous, envious, restricted or unrisen persons, they will most certainly want to hold you down or manipulate you, for that is all they know. Persons can only reflect to you their own state of consciousness, treating you as they treat themselves. No one in right consciousness, in their right God--mind would ever say one negative thing to you, for that would deny the Unlimited Presence and Power of the Light within.

As a civilization, we are still cleaning out. When all have gotten into the fourth dimension, no person on earth will ever receive any negative speculation whatsoever, for all will know each and all is the unlimited manifestation of God. We are sort of sometimes hanging out there and sometimes not. But when we are finally there as a totality, no child will ever hear a disparaging word.

Yet, for now, should you be affronted or challenged regarding the possibilities of your aspiration coming forth ~ you can just say "Thank you for sharing your opinion with me", but know within yourself, "I don't believe it." You don't have to say this directly to anyone, just re-affirm the Truth within. You can if you like and sometimes it is helpful if people are really coming at you in the beginning of your true emancipation to just say,

"Stop telling me that. Just stop. I am not interested".

Whatever you have to do to preserve yourself, is okay. Yet, eventually our affirmations become just a response that is internal, as you say to yourself; "That's not for me". You immediately do not accept any negative speculation into your mental/emotional household, giving it no place to take root in you. For, only that which we actually accept can find entry and take hold.

There is one true story that is just totally so great, and so perfectly illustrates this point. This person was completely,

131

completely paralyzed. Nothing was moving. The doctor finally came to a point where he said: "There is nothing we can do for you." So they took him home to put him in a bed and then to be there until his entire body atrophied and would eventually die.

This individual did not accept this in his spirit. He was still conscious. He did not accept this fate expected for him by others, witnessing his condition. He did not accept it, though totally paralyzed, with nothing, not one thing moving, no evidence of ability to move any limbs, nor any body part.

Within three months, just when he was fully expected to be nearing the end, a little toe started wiggling, then a little time later there began to be movement in one foot and then the entire body reconstituted. He was a runner~ and thereafter, he became one of the greatest runners that ever was. Now whenever you think about this wonderful transformation, defying all odds ~ you will know the power of will and consciousness to move what appears to be even lifeless stuff into a demonstration of total successful life. How great it is that this individual showed forth the power of his indomitable spirit to renew, and all this wondrous regeneration came through his non-acceptance. He didn't decide for that. The doctor said, nothing can be done, but in essence, he said, "I don't care what you say. You don't have a right to decide what is true for me"… and he did his inner work until all of his faculties were working. And so it is that the perfect life of Spirit within him responded to him and the enormity of his courage and faith, reconstituting and bringing into perfect function and full use every aspect.

This is the formidable power of consciousness and Faith in the all-power within. There are endless stories to delight us with transcendent joy and limitless vision of what we may accomplish ourselves, but what you want to realize is that these are real stories and testimonies to Highest Truth. People are really doing this. How are they doing it? Through their undying faith and conviction of the unlimited life of Spirit in themselves.

The well-known author, Walter Starkey, was critically hurt as a horse he was riding threw him and then hit his chest hard, creating so much damage that the doctors said, "Walter you will never walk again", and he was in terrible physical pain. Nevertheless, because he is a man of undaunting Faith, he persisted to know there must be a way and ultimately was Divinely guided to have a Rolphing session, (a technique of deep tissue massage and re-alignment). In spite of excruciating pain, he did not accept that he had no chance to recover, in his spirit giving thanks to the Creator of all that is for the perfect path of recovery, and within two weeks he was out of that bed and within about only a month he was fully walking fine. No impairment. And now, he continues to do just great.

This is the great power of our consciousness, when rightly aligned with all the Divine forces of Heaven and Earth, and most particularly when aligned with Highest Truth, as it was most definitely in Walter's case. It is one thing, when we are trying to accomplish our goals with our human will alone, and not acknowledging God, nor allowing the Infinite to direct. Results will always contain some limitation. But when we affirm; "I am one with that great God cosmos of being, and though no one even supports me right now, I believe there is that to bring me out perfectly and right…at such a time, affirming: "I stand in my word"…a world of good opens unto us. Certainly God loves and responds to all, but one who is so courageously standing out firmly and bravely in Truth ~ is the one who will receive the benefits, far better than one locked in fear, or one trying to accomplish the desired goal merely by their own power. For by the Law of Mind, though the Infinite Capacity be mine to use without limit, I can only receive that which I can accept.

Always be open at the top to receive of the very best, and know for yourself; "I am going and going and going like the energizer battery until I succeed because I am a Divine being, who always overcomes, through complete reliance on the Highest and the Best in me." " I will not let you go, 'til you bless me, Lord!"

People are succeeding all the time. Persons even succeed at failure, if they choose. Nothing that happens in your world is caused by persons, places and conditions on the outer, nothing. Every condition in your life emerges from the inner plane, the world of

Cause. It is so freeing to realize that whatever mind has done, mind can undo.

Take on the new way, and know all you have to do is to remind yourself about that Truth that you are in charge, and already you will be inspired in a new way, realizing you are not a victim at all, and so it is completely up to you. What do you want to live? Do you want to live victimized by past tendencies and beliefs? Ask yourself this regarding all the issues you have written down and noted as most important to you at this time. Take on the new and bountiful Divine Idea there. Exchange fear for Faith, walk the talk, declare only the Presence and Power of God in your situation, and all shall come right.

Ask: *Is this something someone told me or is that something I believe myself?*

And you will be able to distinguish what is collective mind programming which will always pull you down and always cheat you of your greatness, if you buy into it. Make the choice, stand out on God in Faith and make your move. Start to prepare to receive for the thing that you want, by daily envisioning yourself there.

Rather than saying: "Poor me", ~ "Well, I am just sure it won't happen, for it has never before been so"... get busy and if you want the computer to arrive, for example, clean up your desk already, make room for it, get ready. Get ready, for what you want, not for what you don't want.

In this moment, just pick one issue that seems to trouble you the most, and try to formulate a new realization about yourself with regard to that area, that you have pinpointed. Just pick the most major one for now.

Make a new statement of conscious awareness…that you can refer to at any time…a statement of your eternal being that empowers and aligns you with Perfect Truth, i.e. "Because I now know I am one with God, I have a new option for myself, and I make this statement about myself right now and just write out what that is.

For example, "Because I am one with God…I realize that I am healthy, wealthy and successful at all times…I will always be guided in the perfect, right way."

Strive to always preface your statement with ~ "Because I am one with God…I realize _____ (fill in the blanks with your new realization)." This is acknowledging Source, performing the greater conscious alignment, and gives the ultimate reason of why you can so confidently make this statement, again not relying on yourself alone, but indeed, upon the Greater, ever at hand. With such a statement of Unity, all that the Greater is opens unto you. The horizon now lifts to reveal the Presence of perfect solution.

If your area of concern is your work life, your personal life, the health of your body, mind, or soul ~ declare your oneness with the Most High, and realize what this means to you, for there are no limitations in God, therefore, none in you ~ no horizon too great for you to aspire to, no demonstration of transcendent measure that is impossible to you, if you rely upon Source. By relying on the Infinite in you, know the perfection shall always come forth, in the very best possible way and to the most magnificent degree.

No matter what the issue may be, take a breath, and go upstairs in heart and mind, uniting with First Cause, and now the greater attribute is awakened and available to you. (Visit the Five Stages of Treatment, provided in the back pages, to find out more.)

Be specific and apply the attributes and qualities and capacities of the Divine Presence to your every area of concern. Declare the transcendent Divine Principle you are one with, over, above and beyond present conditions. If you are suffering lack, declare the Principle of never-ending Abundance, available for every need. Seek to affirm the Spiritual Opposite of your condition ~ that wholeness, peace and poise of Divine Solution, ever at hand.

"Because I am one with God, I am now restored to perfect health, wealth and well-being." This is consciousness realizing a new possibility, coming to a different conclusion... for now you know you are one with the All, and are claiming your Greater Estate.

Be sure your new realization has no restrictions in it. Whenever doubt or concern surfaces, simply notice that and re-affirm your statement often, putting up reminders around your homes and offices, so you will have ready reference, whenever you slip down in your thinking, feelings, or expectations.

Every mystic knows that "God is my unfailing supply", and becomes the thing that I need. Once realized, you are on your way to the life more abundant, placing your faith in the One Source that will never let you down.

Thus, relying on that which is Greater to aid us in breaking us out of our limitation, brings forth greater fruit, and we help the action along the way, helping God help us, by doing our part, maintaining Faith, regardless of what appears, avoiding negation and consciously thinking in terms of only what we would like to experience...Giving Thanks in Advance and preparing to receive.

Will reaches its ultimate use in service of the Divine. It is the most sublime Divine tool for you to establish the Highest Patterns of Being, right in your everyday life and concerns.

With my will, I can choose what I would like to establish and I can make a decision to carry it through, and then, in the instant, all the vitalizing currents of life flow right into the place where I have made my choice.

For instance, I can say, "Thank you for good health.", and envision myself in that condition. And then, suddenly if I need a vitamin, that will be the thing that shows up. Suddenly, because of my commitment, the way opens and whatever I need appears. I find my way. The right person, place or thing just appears. That is how the individual will joins with the Divine, to bring perfect answers to every prayer. If I know that every perfect and right solution exists simultaneously with the problem, there will be no time where I find myself buying into despair of "no way"

Will reaches its ultimate use when it is aligned with the perfect will of life. And the will of life is to perpetuate that wholeness which it is, in other words, more livingness please. The Divine Will for you any matter can never desire or project diminishment of the life force. Thus it is that my will, aligned with the will of life itself, produces greater and greater experiences for me. And, if what your mind is on is 100% for your beneficent increase, for good of any sort, and it harms no one, and is expressing more life... then you can rest assured you've got a good choice going on, and are perfectly in alignment with all forces of creation.

Always think in terms of more life, more life, expanding your vision of the greatest good you can conceive of, dwelling in the place of the Most High. All possibilities of outcomes in any matter are yours to choose. Daily cultivate richest and most prosperous pictures of your sublime success in perfect harmony and peace.

Now, I will use my will to manifest that which I place my faith in. This is getting to the great Principle of Faith, understanding that Faith is a Law of the Universe and reveals the substance of underlying beliefs. We know that things manifest according to what we believe in. Now, what does that mean? When I believe in something, I place my Faith in it. I put my faith power behind it. Thus, if I believe in "I can't", or I believe in "It's hard", I am placing my Faith in what I don't want to experience. Moreover, even if a thing feels difficult to you, always realize that "There is that within me that is greater and there is no difficulty in God." If you are ever relying on the Greater-in-you and all surrounding, there will be nothing too great for you to accomplish with the Divine at the helm.

Will, backed by faith is a mighty force that shall never be denied. Ask yourself, what am I placing my faith in? And if you find that it doesn't measure up to what you know to be true about the life-force itself, check it, transform it and redirect your Faith in the direction of what you want to achieve. Will and Faith work hand-in-hand in manifesting our every good.

Vision plus velocity of Faith equals certain Victory. Ask yourself, am I placing my faith in Divine Life, in God-in-me, as me, through me, the power of life, in me, as me, through me?, and then using the Divine Gift of will to give substance and direction to the accomplishment of this wonderful thing I have in mind? Am I doing this?" Realize, all of your gifts to accomplish and to overcome are stirred by your Faith. All Infinite capacity is brought into action on the manifest plane by virtue of Faith.

If one believes like Henry Ford, that "I can", even when no resources are in sight ~ you will be supplied all that you need. On some level, Ford was divinely compelled, knowing ~ "I've got an idea whose time has come and this car has got to be made. My Faith will rise above every apparency of obstacle and bring to me everything I need to demonstrate that." Faith is a power...a sublime and mystical power to create whole new worlds. You want to be well forever, and your invincible Faith that your prayers are always answered in perfect right ways will bring you over and above any seeming obstacle or challenge ~ will take you over the seeming barriers, transcendent of that old condition, into the next phase of expansion, supplying all know-how, ways and means.

Faith alone builds new worlds, like Columbus discovering the great land of America. What is Faith? Faith is such a strong belief that anything else is impossible. Any other consideration is impossible. Faith is a power, a transcending power so great that if all things had to change to accommodate the perfect Faith of the one resting in the High Place within, believing in optimum results, so it would be. Mountains would dissolve into the sea, and troubling issues of a life time would be resolved at once.

And we are always having Faith in something, are we not?

The life Transcendent is born of Faith. When there is no resource in sight, Faith goes out there as an active power, with Divine Intelligence guiding, often in ways unknown to conscious mind, finding the perfect right source, the substance and the way.

Thus, to rise to the greatest level of living and understanding that you possibly can, you must will to transcend the cycle of death, defeat, deterioration, illness, and the like. Will to transcend the entire pattern. And place your faith in the supreme power of life to give you every secret you need. Such constant thinking and acknowledging keeps you in perfect alignment with that consummate power. Remember this power keeps all things moving rightly in their spheres. So what is the problem? Can it not produce for us what we have asked? It is the power that has produced worlds. Remind yourself of this, often.

This majestic causal power that literally runs through our very veins and is contained in every breath, is often simply inconceivable to us ~ that great power, which manifest the universe, indeed all universes of being, the cosmos and ourselves. Dwell upon the nature of the Great Reality often, knowing it is yours.

Now ~ when we strike out into new territories we must define our purpose... to give our gifts of Will and Faith direction, define and find our purpose. Live in the consciousness of increase, picturing yourself in greater conditions than ever before.

142

Where do you want your heavenly agents to go, and accomplish for you? What do you want these mighty tools to manifest for you?

And we must not rest upon the proof of the past, yet become living proof of the great unlimited in our very own lives. No more do we relegate the greatest demonstrations to the Masters of the past: "Well they did it, that's nice, but not for me." Yet, we must strive to attain the Great Estate for ourselves. Because I am and you are the only place that God can happen. "Where I am, is the place where Infinite Mind experiences itself." Thus, let us be so thrilled to break through all former barriers for ourselves, based on our supreme soul powers of Faith and Will, and all the rest will follow.

What barrier do you wish to transcend right now through the Immortal Life of God-in-you? What Gift of Divine Measure can take you over every obstacle of the past to certain victory now? Let us soar in new found freedom, taking ourselves to totally new levels by the transcendent power of the Divine within.

TRANSCENDING BARRIERS

Now let us go within... to the place of the Most Holy and the Most High, the place where the Divine and Sacred Self flourishes in eternal peace and joy, the place where all answers to every issue exist.

143

Let each one choose the barrier you most desire to transcend now, knowing there is a perfect Solution of Divine measure and capacity waiting to come forth...to free you forever from this concern, to provide the perfect way up and over into greater fulfillment than you have ever known.

Envision yourself walking a golden road, with each stone magnetically adding more and more energy of accomplishment to you. What are these imperishable stones composed of? What vital and Immortal substance of power does each contain? Is it courage, Wisdom, Truth, Faith, or Divine Love? Is it the belief that there is always the Highest and Best way? Is it the knowledge that the universe is a perfect circle of need and need met in perfection?

Now see yourself passing over every past obstacle in your path, now arriving safely on the shore of your outstanding fulfillment, rich in harmonious and fulfilling surroundings, enjoying every moment of this accelerated state of being, where you are enjoying the fullness of the Divine Self, where all that have you needed along the way has perfectly manifested for you in just the most exquisite Divine Order. Everything that was a part of your great demonstration truly came forth every step of the way.

Now looking back across the bridge of time, ask what was it that you did differently that got you to the place where you are now, so happy and so fulfilled? What person, place, feeling, thought, idea

144

or condition manifested just for you? What change occurred at the critical moment where you would usually have gotten stuck?

What caused you to transcend that familiar barrier, which now is no more?

Now, see yourself transcending and bringing your good through, over and over again, with the new pattern now firmly established in your being. Every time you think of your goal, see yourself there. See yourself well past the obstacle, smoothly arriving at your destiny, with no interruption in your manifestation.

And when all is complete in your mind and heart, return to the present time, knowing you now have the way ~ that shall not fail. The new and Divine element so necessary for your success is now always available to you.

AUM! BLISS!

~

Remember it is not enough to perform the cleansing of feelings and attitudes. That is very important but also we must have vision... to give our life force and energy and give the will and the creative life force a direction.

Dwell upon Divinely Desirable Outcomes always and perfectly right ~ created just for you. Live in the certainty of your good future now. Know there is always a Divine Way to overcome every obstacle, a Higher Substance, Attribute and/or Capacity that shall catapult you to radiant success. Apply these attributes of Divine Solution every time you need.

Regardless of what may be going on ~ know only the perfection of Spirit within, moving past all appearances of affliction, difficulty or delay.

Live by intuition and communing with Heaven's Mind ~ always drawing direct inspiration and guidance from Above.

Now let us see how all things may be healed in the Perfect Light of God.

IMMORTALITY NOW AND FOREVER ~

HOW TO LIVE FOREVER IN YOUR DIVINE BODY OF LIGHT!

CHAPTER TWO

PART II

HOW TO LIVE FOREVER IN YOUR DIVINE BODY OF LIGHT!

~

YOUR SACRED HEALING TOOLS!
"HEALING BODY, MIND, AND EMOTIONS!"
(Converting All to Light and Love!)

CHAPTER TWO
PART II

YOUR SACRED HEALING TOOLS

CONVERTING ALL TO LIGHT & LOVE!!

At any time you may take the light of God and apply it for the healing of any situation. The entire universe, scientifically, is composed of nothing but light, moving molecules...us and everything in it. It is all light in motion, all Divine Substance. And there is no place where God is not, no matter how dense things may have become. In other words, everything is light, and all is Life

In the over-arching umbrella of Light, we have available all the healing substance that we need. The intelligence within the universe exists as light, and we ourselves are the embodiment of that. We may access that flow of light that is always going on at any time and to take the threads of light and sweep it through conditions.

You could hold out your entire subconscious mind mentally, and envision it all be cleaned out by the perfect Light. Mentally view the cleansing action from on High. Hold out the whole thing before your eyes and view all the opinions, attitudes, memories, and everything contained that composes your whole history of thought. Hold it out and just stream the light through it, filling it with white Light.

Remember we spoke of the necessity to clean out our thought atmospheres and at this time we have really done enough work where we don't have to do this transformation bit by bit or item by item, identifying what every single little thing is or has been. Just take the whole thing out. You already know what is in there basically. The subconscious mind is a vast repository of all your beliefs. And the problem is that the subconscious mind is also the creative mind. So unless we clean it out, the contents will act to hold us down and the subconscious then isn't free to create unlimitedly, and doesn't go forward to do all that it can do.

The subconscious possesses the totality of Divine Intelligence and know how, is the maintainer and sustainer of the body, and all vital glands and operations.

When you go to sleep at night, while you are doing your thing, that Divine Intelligence within you is curing the fatigue, is straightening out everything, is regenerating you and doing everything you have requested, on your behalf ~ the perfect servant of conscious mind.

So it is our business to consciously do the best we can to keep it clean of error thought, so it can operate in its original, unhindered manner, free of limited memories, history, collective negative thoughts throughout time. At any time you can just envision the light sweeping through all of mind and taking out all negatives, immersing in the perfect light. You can do this at home daily, at the end of each day, indeed as often as you like. Just understand what I am saying now, that you can just do this clean sweep of everything that has transpired, even unto a moment ago. ..a visualization, where you simply take out what you want to clean.

And you can also do this with any organ, an eye, a lung, your heart or whatever, just bring it out before your inner eye and stream the light of God, through it, visualizing all adjusting and all obstruction dissolving in that great and all-encompassing light.

You can really do this quite effectively, and experience such warmth and relief, from using this ultimate healing tool ~ the Light of God, and what you are doing is simply consciously participating with your subconscious mind…enhancing and re-enforcing what it already knows to do, as well as consciously cleansing, so there are no conflicting thoughts, and this is very powerful to do, rendering swiftest results towards the change you desire.

If you have obstruction anywhere in body, mind or feelings, Divine Light is the one and only thing that heals. God is the only healing action that is. So if you have a body part that is sore or hurting, and you just visualize streaming that light through it and seeing everything harmonizing, soothing, and the light going through, even burning through sometimes, coursing through and breaking up very congested areas, you will begin to feel so wonderful. It is a great healing tool and you can do that with your body, with your emotions, indeed, with your whole subconscious mind. This mind contains all the memories you have stored, all the judgments and opinions, and beliefs you have held, but greater than all of these, this mind also contains the Perfect Patterns and memories of your Divine Self, as pure Divine Light, a radiant star in the firmament.

Most times I simply use pure white light, but some like to use different colors of the spectrum including the very transformational violet flame.

At times, I will just take a moment and course it through my whole body, and it has a way of easing all of the muscular structure, the tissues, adjusting the heart beat to the perfect rhythm of the universe, aligning all with the flow of Divine breath and life ~ and I will include in such times all that needs healing, deeply penetrating all with that laser light, wherever it needs to be, 'til the point where I can actually physically feel its beneficent and healing effect.

Now, if we know that that every organ has a Divine function, and is the embodiment of a perfect pattern of a Spiritual Idea, such as heart represents the perfect flow of love, the digestive system represents perfect inflow and outflow, the circulatory system ~ perfect motion without any stagnation whatsoever ~ when healing, we can not only give thanks in advance that this perfect Spiritual Pattern is manifesting, knowing such instruction is being immediately acted upon by the Divine Mind via our subconscious creative capacity, we can then help God help us re-align by sweeping the Light through and witnessing the transformation into perfection, with our inner eye.

What we ever so joyously realize is our complete, inherent capacity to heal and adjust any and all things. Once we are understanding mind and how it works, we realize that everything takes place on the invisible planes of consciousness, and that everything that was ever created in the manifest world, just like the wonder of the laser beam, is the outer symbol of the actual inner activity that is always taken place. We then can know the right order of things, and can proceed consciously to create and perform necessary corrections, independently of history, even healing existent conditions, from within out.

When you swirl that Light of Divine Love all around and through your circumstances and relationships, a wonderful alchemy occurs.

As wonderful as it is, even the laser is only a symbol of the great Light within. We don't have to depend upon a laser. We don't have to depend upon any system of outer healing, because we already have the entire system, already within. Though we may greatly enjoy the use of the outer, realize the fountain of Light you already are and possess. Do understand that you have it all, the Allness of the Light and of God at your disposal at all times…for any good purpose of healing yourself under Heaven. And, we have the Kingdom of the Holy Breath. Deep breathing revitalizes all your cells in the instant, filling with the complete love, light and substance of God.

And so we can have direct access to these riches for Divine Healing and for maintaining longevity, as long as desired. At night, the creative healing power flows free and unhindered by your concern of the day, ready to create a better tomorrow for you. Before you go to sleep is the most perfect time to Give Thanks for the healed conditions you desire and to give thanks that it is so, not wondering how. As you drift off in Gratitude, it is also a wonderful time to envision the Light of Love, working throughout all. For example, if I go to bed and something is going on in my body, I just simply take time to do a meditation bringing in Divine Light. And I will stream the light through whatever part of my body is hurting, as well as deep breathing, breathing in the breath of God. Deep breathing energizes you, bringing all into perfect comfort, balance and peace. Breathe in seven, hold seven, and then release and blow out to the count of seven all that has gone before, emptying completely, and then I will do my light work on myself. Then, I simply release myself from any concern after I feel that I'm comfortable enough, and have restored myself enough, and I visualize, visualize, visualize ~ really consciously directing the Light very specifically through an area that is really thick…If a muscle has gotten tight, just streaming that light through, forwards and backwards, through and through the tissues, 'til I see the musculature loosening and aligning.

Be aware that this Divine Intelligence works all night when we are sleeping, that those Divine workers and agents of Creation are at work. Put in your order and give thanks that whatever needs to be removed is removed, whatever needs alignment is aligned, whatever needs perfecting is made so, and give thanks that you wake up feeling just wonderful.

Just center in Gratitude for the healing you desire, whether for conditions of body or outer circumstances: "Thank you that I wake up and I have no pain, whatsoever. Thank you for doing that for me." The intelligence in the universe knows very well, how to restore you like that, and is perfectly able and happy to align, mend and perfect anything for you; whether it be the restoration of the luster of your skin, the sublimely perfect function of your organs and glands, the dissolution of any congested areas, or the transformation of a body cell to its luminous inherent Light.

Lord knows how to maintain, restore and resurrect all that the Divine has created, and has equipped you with its own entirely Divine and Intelligent system.

After I have achieved a state of harmony and peace, it is then that I turn my requests for body's well-being over to that which knows how. I release my own will to the Highest Will of Good, after I have done my own work at the conscious level, by establishing right ideas of spiritual prototypes, giving thanks, working the God-given Light; and then, in deep gratitude, I turn all over to the Divine Intelligence within, entrusting the job to all those heavenly workers to do whatever is needed in terms of my body maintenance, knowing I have placed my goals for myself in the very best hands, none other than the Divine Creator itself.

To achieve optimum states of physical well-being, I highly recommend this daily practice, knowing the subconscious is your best friend, the one that never says no, and it will take up your request for whatever you ask it to do, and it will go and do it straight away.

While you are resting, there is not a lot of ego noise and chatter, or distraction to obstruct the action. That is why you can put in a simple request accompanied by your statement of Gratitude, and have your prayers answered so beautifully and with ease. If you have a cut on the hand, just say: "Thank You, it is already healing.

155

Wow, thank you that you are already taking care of it and it is already mending and well on the way... tomorrow when I wake up." This method provides healing really rapidly. The subconscious mind is connected with God and it knows how, whereas, at the level of personal will we might be stuck in notions of time, limitation, I can't(s), or impossibilities, feeling things are difficult, whereas the Universal subconscious mind, the Great doer of all things, doesn't know any obstructions at all.

A fellow was burned very badly in a fire and fortunately the doctor who rushed to the site of this emergency was very knowing of a profound Truth. He understood that if he could communicate with the subconscious mind of his patient within a very short window of time, following this horrific incident ~ he would not suffer burns. Thus, he spoke to the patient's heart, while he was still in a near comatose state. This was within a half an hour from the time the incident happened, and he was literally burned all over, and the doctor just said some profoundly healing words to his patient, knowing the power of the subconscious mind. "You are perfect, you are healing just great. There is nothing wrong with you. There is no scar tissue. You are going to be just fine." As the doctor continued to affirm his patient's perfection, that patient healed entirely, very rapidly; whereas somebody who was laden down with collective mind thinking of time, impossible(s) and delays, severity of the situation, might have never healed and might be carrying around very heavy scar tissue for the rest of their days. We never want to limit the Infinite healing capacity, and we want to understand how it works on subconscious, unseen levels.

So that is so incredible and so wonderful to know, and a power to be eternally grateful for, one that can raise you above every condition and trauma like it never happened, just by virtue of deep conviction and heart-felt gratitude ~ the very same force that could and did re-build this gentleman's body, can also do that for you

.

If you are taking care of your body temple every day in this way; checking it out, how does it feel, asking for what restorative action you want, giving thanks to the Divine Intelligence that it does the work; then you will never deteriorate. It would be impossible for you to do so, for you are living in concert with the Divine, always maintaining your life and conditions at optimum levels, receiving the benefits of right maintenance.

Remember that Light is the one and only thing that heals and that can heal in permanence, establishing within you the Immortal Body of Light. Light and Love are the one and only quintessential life giving properties that have ever healed anything, the Light of Mind, the Heart of Love. It may look like a pill, but the reason the pill works is because you believe in the pill.

Therefore, you can say that you do love that pill, and you have placed your faith in it, knowing the whole power of God itself is at work....a very wise thing to do, if you want to experience completely healing. In the instant, you have given the pill complete access to work.

Light and Love, clearly, are the vital powers, the one and only elements that are empowered from above to heal absolutely anything and everything. Your belief is the power that ignites the force. And, life knows itself completely, knows how to do the whatever for you.

Just know that any time you need, you have this world of Immortal, renewing, restoring and rejuvenating wonder before you, and I recommend establishing new habits of right maintenance. This would be to do your light meditations, daily taking your area of issue ~ bringing it out in front of your mind's eye, streaming light over, in, around and through it again and again, penetrating the subcutaneous levels, until it seems that all is right. And then, simply let go and let the perfection work.

In a sense you might call this a form of Mental surgery, spiritual surgery, using the perfect and all-inclusive white light of the Universe to cleanse, and then infilling with pure Divine substance, rich in every vital nutrient you require.

Now when you take out negatives from your subconscious mind, envision burning out, eliminating, releasing, converting and dissolving any patterns of negation, remembering that you have that light to heal and convert whatever accumulation of negation that is in there, whether it came from a million years ago or from right now... and so, in that constant cleansing action and vigilance, you are living trace free, baggage free. Every new day is a wonder to behold.

If you do not do this constant cleansing there can be accumulation going on, and old, unfinished stuff constantly coming in. Apply your tools of conscious conversion, and if you don't have time to sit down and figure it all out at any given moment, just ask that Christ mind, that great mind within you, to heal all that negation...and to replace with the fountain of never-ending Truth.

Do this Divine Healing process as often as you want to, until it's just an ongoing moment to moment habit, but for deep contemplation, at least once a day, truly taking time out. Apply the Great Healing Light whenever you feel the need. Remember you don't have to know all the details, all the wherefore (s) and why (s).You can simply ask the great and all-encompassing mind, the Christ mind, the cosmic mind within you ~ to remove whatever; so that it no longer disturbs you.

Once we have healed ourselves of the tendency to believe that we have to deteriorate physically and that we will have to die, that we are not in charge, that we cannot pick our times and our places of our own volition, what have we got then? Nothing less than a pure body of light exists now, for that is all that there is and the ever-regenerating light is now flowing without obstruction. All that there is 'is' varying degrees of light, light flowing or light obstructed. Light is what consciousness looks like, what we look like, now, and this pure body of light you have right now is 100% total God substance, a perfect symmetry of beauty, harmony, circulation, order and transparency. Not transparency in terms of disappearing, but in terms of the fineness of Divine Life it exudes. Every aperture radiates light. There is nothing closed off.

Let us take a moment now to do another exercise and meditation to help incorporate this powerful, majestic healing tool…to meet your perfect Body of Light within.

HEALING ALL THINGS PHYSICAL

Let us once again, come in to the center of being, putting all thoughts out of mind, leaving all that has passed even until a moment ago, behind… Moving now into that sacred Temple of Light and Peace, your own place of communing with the Most High.

Now, in this Temple of your Divine Self, I would like you to locate your perfect Body of Light, and once you have found it, I would like you to look at it and realize that this great body of Light is the actual Divine Pattern of you… now manifest completely and

160

free, and see that it has total self-expression of all the Divine Qualities that it embodies, the total radiance of God, Highest Love and Light.

This is the entire potential of you fully realized. Remember now, this, your own body of Light, is the Divine Pattern of you... God's perfect idea for you, richly fulfilled.

Now see that this Body of Light is generating a tremendous current of energy toward you, surrounding you and then enfolding you in the great power of Light, which you are receiving and absorbing and luxuriating in. Now realize this perfect pattern of you always moves before you in consciousness, guiding your way here and there. See how it is streaming the Light of God through its every aspect, every function, every tissue, every cell. See how it knows what to do. Recognize in this instant you can do this too, and this is the idea for you and you are free and you can regenerate on the Light any time you want and use it to perfect and restore each and every body part that requires, each and every brain cell, each and every blood cell, each and every cell of thought. See the light of pure Spirit now flowing through your own body, flowing through your own cells, through your skeletal structure. How wonderful it is to be perfectly aligned.

Feel that light encompassing you as the skeletal structure, as the marrow, as the tissue, as all that is... and behind this form is a very beautiful form of the DNA pattern of your Divine being. And you see that this pattern is radiating with the Light of God and every point of Light in it represents a Divine and Transcendent Quality and exudes the Light of that particular quality into each and every form.

See the light coursing through your beautiful skin, which is the cloak around the structure of God. See how your skin is radiating and rejoicing and flowing the life of God throughout the whole form. Now, see your whole form as light, a frame of light, the activity of light, the intelligence, the harmony, the inter-connectedness, the flowingness of Divine order and action... and now see yourself rising Higher in consciousness, forever overseeing perfect maintenance of your body. You are maintaining eternal and unmatched well-being through your perfect understanding that body is indeed the perfection of Spirit, the Light of Spirit and First Cause... ageless, timeless, eternally sustained, perfect being.

Draw upon that Infinite Light now for any part specifically that requires restoration.

As you bring up that situation that needs adjustment, see the light charging and streaming and coursing through... breaking up all crystallization, arranging and restoring each and every molecule to perfection. Breathe in the breath of perfection and relief that the Light is doing the work.

Tell your body and every organ and aspect, and cell, gene and all that you love it and you recognize it is wholly a Spiritual Idea of Perfection. And you thank Divine Intelligence and Infinite workers of Light for maintaining your body perfectly, eternally. You right now recognize it is 100% full Spiritual Substance in all ~ the wholeness made manifest. Your body is a perfect Body of Light and Divine Substance and Form.

In this wholeness now you choose to forgive and release any past idea of imperfection, you release any idea that endless life needs to stop ever. You promise yourself you shall continue indefinitely and as long as you are able to rightly maintain the health of your body in Light and Love and Right Recognition.

See body's susceptibility to you, see how perfectly malleable and unfixed it is... That perfect Substance of Spirit is always responding to you. Now release and Thank God for this beautiful Light of Life that is yours... that you can use anytime, anywhere, and thank God that you can move into your Immortal Body of Light any time. Realize God has given you all, all along and all-in-all, and when you feel perfectly regenerated and at ease, return to the present, remembering the experience you have had and how to re-create it any time you need.

Immersing in the Light always brings joy and causes our Spirits to shine.

One pathologist remarked she actually took the brain out in studying physical pathology, but never had known she could do this mentally to great effect, indeed altering brain patterns.

Another realized those points of light in the radiant Light Body of the Divine Pattern, are indeed equal to those acupuncture points that get stimulated, when receiving treatment. When you go in there with the actual light, you trigger those points of alignment, re-aligning the flow of life force (chi), and from here, you can do whatever you need to do.

So I suggest you do this often on your own in a similarly meditative form or however you want to do it. and be sure that you are informing your subconscious that you are changing your structure to reflect what it is in God, and that you want it to assist you in now removing from your body temple anything that is obstructive, harmonizing and transforming any part of your organs, skeletal structure, circulatory system, or anything that needs healing… cleansing, removing, healing the whatever, and that you are bringing in the balance and harmony with and by that Divine Light, instead. This is called light maintenance.

As Light centers around the chakras, there will be a simultaneous opening up of the great fan of existence, accompanied by deep peace and release… and I also recommend that after you do your work, that you then always release it to the great even Higher

Intelligence to complete the job for you. The Divine has ways and means far beyond the ken of ordinary mind.

Strive to really know your direct relationship with Light, and be sure that you are always telling yourself the Truth of Light, realizing that you as consciousness are now giving your own subconscious the new information that will go forth to form new prototypes for your world of experience, reforming the pattern to make it the way you want it to be, ultimately to conform to your Highest Divine Pattern of ever-sustaining life.

For right maintenance, meditate, every single day. If you are serious about this, you must meditate and enjoy times of deep breathing. Meditate upon whatever Divine Quality you would like to activate, enhance, and release as an action into your life.

Choose whatever Divine Quality you want to release as an action in your life, such as Joy or Faith, or Infinite Abundance. Whatever you want to release into your life, just meditate on the Divine Words and take a receptive position, i.e. "God is perfect Abundance, and I am too!" Or. "The Perfect Abundance of God surrounds me always." And as you meditate on the Divine Idea, information will come to you and also the alchemical re-alignment will occur, and the re-arrangement of your entire body structure will happen too, as you simply receive and absorb whatever comes to mind. As you come into such peace within, your entire body, blood

165

pressure and all will begin to harmonize as never before (even acidic fluids turning to benevolent substance), for you have struck the chords of the Universal harmony and are becoming one., no longer out of sorts.

Keep it very simple… no big deal, meditate on Perfect Peace, perfect Faith, whatever it is that you want, Perfect Supply, "Divine Supply is Perfect", and just say these words gently over and over, and let the information come up for you.

Realize that you charge up every atom of being, when you breathe in the Divine Breath of God (the sacred substance of all of life) , and that opens up everything, so much so that you are, in the instant, sublimely re-vitalized And realize, the power of this breath in this Light is such that it doesn't know any limit. It is perfectly capable of doing the whole thing that needs to be done at any given moment, and cleaning the house instantly, so to speak ~ and if you will allow.

Realize the power of it all, the riches of the Kingdom that are truly yours. Then there is the very important cleansing of the subconscious mind, freeing it of all the erroneous information we have unwittingly given to it, daily cleansing and aligning thought with Truth, Faith and Love, performing right maintenance, cleaning your subconscious mind. There is only a belief that stands between you and your every aspiration, only these hidden negatives thoughts and feelings that drive us towards death. If you are experiencing frustration, realize on some level, you have accepted limitation, and of course anything accepted in mind must record in the body.

What we are doing is really what you could call the ultimate de-programming. Rather, we are going into the Divine programming, lifting all this stuff off, that the Divine Self may be free.

Your feeling life is also of utmost importance, thus strive to maintain harmony and maintain peace, knowing that the very first thing in any troublesome situation one needs to do is to get into harmony. You can run rack and ruin over your physical household and your mental household when you permit agitation to go on. Peace is power. Without peace, there is no power.

It is our responsibility to know we that we always have an option to move into peace, regardless of whatever may be going on… and from there, we can then ask for Guidance, for Right Action to be revealed, how to best handle whatever issue, but we must come into Peace first. Nothing can hinder us then, for Peace, Joy and Faith stabilize the great power of our emotions, releasing them to be a mighty constructive force in our worlds.

Yet, with emotions unchecked, unconverted into Love and run awry, we can really accelerate deterioration. That is another way we can guarantee ourselves a lot of aging lines and a host of other maladies, a whole host of physical problems because we have allowed this agitation, which disturbs all the chemistry of the body. Alright, so no more allowing that; you put yourself first and say: "Regardless of what they did, let me come into peace first and I'll find out how to handle it after, in perfect right ways. Let me find a way to forgive as fast as possible, and once again center in the Perfect Truth of Divine Love."

Maintaining your peace is very important, meditation is very important, putting you in higher alpha and theta states, moving you out of the normal vibrational level into the Higher, where Divine Inspiration flows. That is why you feel so rested when you come out of meditation and your 144,000 nerves need this alignment. Meditation calms and centers the nerves. When it is said that the great ones are coming, and there are 144,000 in number... Guess where they are? Within your own nervous system, and moments of silent communion perform an exquisite alignment, an attunement with the Highest and the Best in you. Peace aligns your nerves.

As an additional benefit, your breathing equalizes, once again in tune with the universal harmony of the spheres... and your heart rate slows down and wonderfully stabilizes, bringing a flow of warmth and well-being. By making Peace your goal, no matter what appears, you are rightly conserving on the life force, as well. Breathe in the Peace and Power that is yours.

When you meditate, you are not over using your vital energies, like when you allow yourself to become very agitated, where you are spilling out the life energy, all caught up in turbulent emotion, over-using Divine Light energy. Meditation gives you that empowering centeredness, that Peace that surpasseth all understanding, and allows life to flow through you in a harmonious manner, a very nurturing manner, and you become infinitely strong, indeed.

There is another wonderful method of transformation that you can daily use for great Spiritual Advancement every day, and this process has to do with emotional cleansing which is very important for eternal life.

Knowing how important it is to sustain the Divine state of inner quietude, one realizes how imperative it is to daily align through maintaining non-disturbance and a state of imperturbability. Finding ways to exist at the Highest Levels of Divine Love is key to right maintenance of the emotional body. So everyday what I do is I run the movie of my day. I learned to do this some time ago. This unfailing method was given to me in a moment of inspiration, just came to me at a strong point in my desire to evolve in my emotional life.

At a major period of my life, I was wondering how to cleanse all these feelings that we accumulate all day long, when someone isn't nice to you or someone fails you or a situation doesn't measure up. Realize, when we go to sleep with all these residue feelings left unresolved and weighing upon us, we go to sleep like we are laden with luggage that weighs a lot. And it surely weighs us down, increasing the weight of karma, accumulating more and more attachment to unwanted conditions, really bogging the Divine Soul down. So instead of continuing on the same old way ~ I appealed to the Greater in Me to give me a way ever-up and ever-out: "God, there has got be a way to live where you are releasing karmas and not creating new karmas and causes and effects as you go along. There must be a way where you can become lighter and lighter as you live, more and more loving and able to not wake up with your luggage every morning."

That surely makes it hard to get out of bed, doesn't it?

It was then that a Divine Technique was given to me whereby one can begin to live trace-free, where you will find weight and encumbrance steadily leaving you and dropping away, as it did me.

Even though I have always loved life ~ There was a time, when it would take me at least two hours to get fully up and ready to to face my day, for residue of unresolved emotions remained. I just had to have my coffee, and often found myself not wanting to go to do this or do that, all such tendencies to delay and procrastinate arising from conflict in the emotional field. In spite of my natural great energy and enthusiasm for life, still the sluggish start would periodically appear. Now I want to tell you that by steadily using this technique, there is no difference between waking and sleeping to me. I get up and I am truly up and ready to go, enjoying a seamless transition from morning to night. When I go to sleep, I sleep like a baby. There are no more heavy transitions, because there is no more accumulation going on. I have been cleaning out for a long time and daily continue this process, for I decided that above all I truly want and cherish my Spiritual Freedom, and now, this process has just become the wonderful, natural way to be.

And, you too may enjoy the liberty of doing this technique I was so blessed to receive. You may do this every evening, and before you go to sleep tonight, and then eventually try to come to the place where, in the very moment that you go off balance with even the most slightest negative feeling arising, you will notice that and be able to instantly detach: "Oops. Let me align that." "Let me replace that with a thought of Love, that my soul may rise free."

And then you can go on your way totally whole and doing well.

Realize that just as when we enter the realm of meditation, we have the Divine Option to literally step outside ourselves, and we can take the observer position and look at what we are planning, what we are doing, and from this vantage point perform all the changes we want, so too, we can bring up the movie of the day and play it, run it through our mind's eye, observing one's self as a character in a play. Run the activity of the day through your mind, and see and find the areas where you feel there are still unresolved issues. For instance, when you do this review, you may find that you are still angry at someone, you still have some disappointment, you still want things to have gone another way. Left unresolved, these feelings will compound, causing even more angst, and there you are the next day carrying over the heavy luggage of your experience, yet, you want to live every moment trace free.

So this is very powerful and a very enjoyable method to use. If you do this every day you will start to live trace free of luggage, of baggage. You know how when we wake up it sometimes is like having a hangover. All the memories, all the stuff, all the feelings wake up with us, all those residue emotions that we haven't resolved. And also you can do this for the healing of trauma of any kind, anywhere, entirely releasing traumatic events from your memory and from every cell. There is no time in God, thus healing at the moment you become aware, heals it forever.

CLEANSING THE EMOTIONS

So let us each one in this moment, just get very relaxed, and take a few deep breaths, breathing in the breath of God, filling our

172

being, and releasing; exhaling anything we do not wish to keep or make a part of us. Let us each just go within right now, and get very still going to the center of centers, the Highest of the High, rising to the summit of consciousness. Let us each one now step out gently of our body's shell to overview ourselves, our day, like we are watching a movie... Playing the movie of the day.

In this perfect God space, I would like each one now to go into your personal library of recorded experiences, your file and pull out the roll of film for today, and I'd like you now to go in your mind's eye to place this in the projector and sit down and have a comfortable seat. And now, run the movie of the day before your eyes and as you are looking at it, see if there is anything in there that you need to change, transform to light, come into peace with?

Ask ~ "Is there any condition, any person, place, event, anything at all that I still have disturbance about? That I am still in anger over or have quandry about? Some event?... or do I still have residue feelings about something that someone did? Are there any feelings of hurt, anger, unforgiveness, fear, guilt or doubt, yet lingering and causing pain or frustration?"

"Is there anything I have not perfected in Love this day? Anything I have not come into harmony with this day?" Realize, all things of the world have come to pass, and the Divine-in-you has come to stay. You are building the Immortal Body of Love within.

173

And now, within your mind, come in closer and view that most significant scenario point which needs your attention. Look at that situation, look how you were really feeling in that and perhaps are still feeling that same way now. What do you want to happen there? How would you like to see yourself responding, from the Divine Point of view?

Tune in closely to that situation, seeing yourself in the feeling. Seeing all of the persons and things that have to do with that. How were you then? How are you still feeling about that? Now remember this. Every moment, every thought adds unto you, frees you or causes delay and restriction.

You know that unresolved matter shall form an encumbrance for you and become a hindrance to your own well-being. Thus, for your own well-being, decide you would rather release it, harmonize with it and within yourself, so you can be free, every moment free. For, you certainly desire your freedom above all.

Decide right now as you are perusing this situation, looking at it on the film of your day ~ What do you want to take with you into your tomorrow? That feeling, that bondage there, or God and Love?

What do you want to take onward on your Infinite Journey with you, as an empowerment to your Eternal Life? Every time you are willing to let go and to exchange a negative thought/feeling to

Divine Love, you rise one step Higher, one step freer, as all associated karmas disappear.

Remember you have a choice in the handling of this matter, and can make a choice for Higher Destiny, for the freedom of your Eternal Soul. What do you want to remember about yourself...the glory of God-in-you, the perfect overcomer or something else? What do you want to claim unto yourself about this situation? ~ that you are the Victory of Divine Love conquering all, or the victim of holding on?

Now, ask yourself, "What do I need to do now in mind or heart to establish myself where I want to be? To re-establish the currents of Divine Love? What can I do? What is the thing I need to do?"

Now, whatever you need to do in mind or heart to reconnect and establish the currents of Love...do this now from your spot in this chair looking at this movie. Go and dissolve this matter by the power of God in you, from your memory. Use a Spiritual Tool. Shall it be Forgiveness, Having Faith or Courage, or just knowing there is that in you which is greater, guaranteeing you your right and perfect success in perfect ways. If you know that all of the Love of the Universe is with you, as you earnestly strive to release, what matters a single affront, a moment of frustration? God is with you and supports you all the way.

175

Now see yourself in that same situation doing the new thing. See yourself handling this from the new High Point, letting the old thought pattern or feeling dissolve downstream, nevermore to be a part of you. How are you now? How do you feel now? When you look back at any time on this scenario, any time ever again, how are you now going to remember yourself?

Note how great everything is, now perfected in Love, how all things have come together for greatest good, and you are freely moving on in joy.

Notice the change ~ how you are feeling now? Now, if you were to replay this film or whenever you look back to this time, this spot ~ what are you going to remember now? What do you choose to put into your Divine memory bank now? Once you feel comfortable that you *have truly established the change, know that you now have the perfect tool for maintaining Highest Peace and Love that you can always use to set yourself free.*

And when you are ready, take this information with you and return to the present.

Did you experience any changes in that? Did you get any insight as to how you could see the thing differently? Try and incorporate this method of detaching from the force of residue emotions and viewing from the High Point of View. And, for the least little bit of whatever, if you yet are unable to release it, unable to change it, or yet can't forgive it, ask that Higher Divine Consciousness in you to help you to do that…realizing that holding on to things, for even a moment, is literally retarding your life force.

So it is that we must accomplish everything in Love. And, we must free, we must release, we must forgive so that our life is free to move on in greater glory.

There are a multitude of processes, where you can deepen this method. But leave it to say if you can make it a goal for yourself that every night you want to remember to align all in your day with Love, and you don't want to go to sleep without doing this cleansing, you will be taking a mighty quantum leap in blessing your life so profoundly. And, if you can't do it, for any reason, feeling: "No, I can't let go of that. I can't", as you ask to be able to find a way, you will be able to. And you will wake up lighter and lighter and lighter and lighter. And this technique will really become a new way of being, evolving into an immediate way of addressing any and all circumstances for you…as you begin to live "Heaven on Earth."

The more you use these mighty accelerating tools, you will come to a place where you are releasing and converting automatically, every moment throughout your day, and if you get stuck, you will know how to consciously center within and apply the change. Realize you are not any of the events or conditions that have happened to you, yet something far greater capable of transcending and healing all. I do this process faithfully every night because I realize that if I do not align everything, moment to moment in my life with Highest Love I am just creating karma, baggage, and burdensome attachments, rather than walking the path of Dharma and Grace. So I made the decision at some point and I really would go through this process. I would view everything of the day and if I found any traces there, I would find a way to heal it, for the sake of building my Immortal Body of Light and Love.

As you proceed in transforming your consciousness, you will see that we keep getting the experiences in different clothing, until we have actually done what we need to do, until the transformation is actually complete. If your desire is sincere and you truly want to heal above all else, you will find something to use... A Divine tool empowering you to harmonize difficult situations, to heal whatever came up and to be able to accomplish your very worthy task. Only ask for assistance from your Divine Self.

Perhaps you will use the Light, sweeping the Light of Love over, in, around and through all. Perhaps, if you encountered a frustrating situation ~ instead of remaining angry at someone who did not do what they said they would, you can just bless them and let it go, knowing that on some level only Perfect Divine Order is taking place. It doesn't matter what tool you use, so long as you are grounded in Higher Principles of the Divine-in-you. Realize how important Love is to you. And, once you are aligned or even desirous of doing so, in the clear space, you can then put in your request of how you would like the next day to be for you, with nothing holding you down. This is living progressively upward into the Greater and Greater Light of Being. This is cultivating the strength and beneficence of the Divine You.

This is a very great thing to do, because if you don't take quality time to maintain your condition of Love, certainly those residue feelings will become luggage, and when you go into your next day, these traces still linger on and bog you down, and they pile up and congeal, and before you know it you've got clogged arteries.

This is the very deepest root of where many of these undesirable conditions of physical problems come from. So you are the one who gets the freedom and reaps the immense benefit by making Highest Love at all times your goal.

If something is still agitating, try again, as long as you need to cleanse from your very soul, and it is very good to ask yourself, "What do I want to take with me?" Remember whatever you are taking with you in mind and heart, you are accumulating to your soul, to your consciousness. That is called karma, cause/effect.

And, at this stellar point, we want our cause/ effect patterns to be in accordance with the Divine Self, positive and life-giving and affirming in every way. We don't want to accumulate negative bondage. We want to throw all of that off now, and choose the Higher Path.

With your commitment to truly live at the levels of Highest Love that you can, you are now choosing to release the lesser for the greater, and for your complete joy on every level. Choosing to be that Love just pays off so immensely ~ so get the art of constant releasing, and forgiving... doing whatever it is you have to do to maintain your peace, and if you can't, if you find yourself still in agitation, then just ask your God self to somehow get you free of that, and when you are sleeping, the answer will come. As long as you know that your greater goal is the recovery of your true Spiritual Identity in God...and that what you are doing now is using every Spiritual Tool you have to gain your own liberty for your eternal soul, you can never go wrong.

If you want the Best in life to be yours, this path is for you... so that you don't have to run around with weights on your feet, and bricks on your heart, so that you can reclaim your Immortal Inheritance in the here and now.

You can utilize this technique for last week, for your entire life, or for any point whatsoever in your own timeline. Since there is no time in the Infinite, the correction will just be successfully made in all time and space, and, once corrected, the past is instantly dissolved from all of mind and being. Sometimes I just run a fast view, a fast replay of my life and take a little checkup, where troublesome spots remain.

If an issue is not resolved, ask yourself; What is really bothering you? Maybe you can light on what it is and then you will be able ~ once you see it, to recognize it as some form of separation from your Source. When you see the Truth of the thing that is really bothering you, you will be able to release it, for all negative thoughts and feelings are based in some type of lie.

For instance if you find that you are still angry at an event, for example, a loved one left, one might ask: "Why would I be angry at them?" And, you will find that underneath that anger is always something else. Perhaps, you are feeling "Now I am alone", or "There will never be another" might be one common thought that could arise. Then I can ask of my God self; "Is that true?" Of course, if we are centered in Truth, we know that Love never runs out, though the form may change, and that is Truth.

You can then work your way out of anger by claiming the Truth every time the feeling arises, and then blessing that person to go on to their good as well.

As you study Divine Principles and learn how to do Treatment, your foundations in Truth will become all that you know, and you will live in the exalted consciousness of Perfect Principle all the time. All Universal Principles reflect a self-existent universe of completeness and wholeness beyond imagining, always available to each and every one.

While persons are going for such magnificent change, we need to hear the Truth, and we need to hear it a lot, and I do hope that throughout this chapter, you have found some of the Secrets to Immortal Life, and Living your Immortality now, as well as methods to successfully sustain.

Always take time out to see yourself in your Immortal existence, a shining star in the heart of God. How did you get to be so fantastic? What did you do? Remember you are as Immortal now as you shall ever be, you only need to bring it out and cultivate the Divine Light body within.

So let it be!
Aum! Bliss!

IMMORTALITY NOW AND FOREVER ~

HOW TO LIVE FOREVER IN YOUR DIVINE BODY OF LIGHT!

CHAPTER THREE

CELEBRATING YOUR IMMORTAL ESSENCE

~

"EXTENDING YOUR LIFE INDEFINITELY!"

CHAPTER THREE

CELEBRATING YOUR IMMORTAL ESSENCE

EXTENDING YOUR LIFE INDEFINITELY!

When we truly embrace our Immortality, it is like giving birth to ourselves, our Infinite Selves, our True Nature.

In this sense, indeed we are all mothers of ourselves, whether we are female or male. Thus, let us breathe deeply and go within for a moment. Let us take a moment to facilitate that birth ~ to prepare the way of that birth by letting go of all concepts, all mind activity, all thought, all definitions.

In a spectacular novel on Creation by Eugene E. Whitworth (Genesis: The Children of Thoth) ~ the inhabitants of the original planet underwent the most intense soul purification and training of their mental and physical bodies in order to successfully project their light bodies anywhere in the universe. As the West Sun drew nigh, scorching the desert plains, a second sun that had appeared and

184

threatened immanent extinction, they needed to be ready at optimum levels, so that they could jettison themselves at will and experience the pure birth on a distant planet of Ayer-Earth. In the culminating moment, the entire civilization dematerialized and successfully transported themselves to the destined planet, where civilization would begin again. And, so it is with us that any time we want to rise ~ the way to the next level is always through cleansing and aligning with the Greater Divine Self. In such true expansion, liberty is attained. And so it is that men become Gods and Gods become men. Genesis records the incredible history of the sacred children of Thoth from the beginning, when despite any obstacle, through sacred immortal practices, Divine Destiny was achieved.

As one spiritual master once said, "If you can name it, that isn't it." So let us put aside calling it something, and let us just empty. Empty and be full... Letting go of all old concepts and ways... Going beyond the body, beyond the emotions, beyond the physical and mental, deep within to our soul, and remain there as the beholder of Truth.

Allow your soul to influence you as you empty and let go. Say softly to yourself, "I am now an empty vehicle of light. I am imbued with a blanket of grace. I allow grace to move me, allow grace to do its business, and to raise me up. I enter the Kingdom within, because of Grace. Grace is the open door, and I allow the Dove of Grace to serve me completely in this holy moment.

I let go of mind, I let go of might, and I allow Grace to be, to sustain me as I am blanketed by it. And I live by it. My thoughts are gone. All judgment has ceased. And I move by grace. I am the beholder of infinite wonder. I am the beholder of Truth. And I put aside all notions. And I just am. I allow spirit to teach. I let Spirit lead. And I put aside all that needs to be put aside. I now have ears to hear. I now am ready to receive. I am empty, and I am Gratitude.

And so, the ascension continues…to loftier heights than ever known.

Thank you, Father Mother God.

And when you feel truly centered and open to Greater Truth than you have ever known, return to the present, ready to receive. Centering meditations are so wonderful. As we all know, before we begin to move into any action, the most important thing we can do is center ourselves because without centering, without quietude, we cannot access our Spiritual core and Ultimate Source of power.

I cannot overstate how important periodic centering in meditation is ~ for the Dove of Divine Grace to appear…to always be open at the top to receive of Divine Influx, to be able at a moment's notice to release all from even a moment ago. I have truly come to the place where, before I take any action whatsoever ~ whether it is picking up the telephone to call and say, "Hi," to a friend, or something far more important ~ I get centered and declare that mighty Presence and Power at hand, which, once contacted, always blesses us immeasurably.

This is truly the greatest expansion of Spirit we have embarked on. Know the spirit of the great Cosmic Mother is shining her love and light over, in and around, through each and every one of us… That each may receive of the greatest and most profound awakening and illumination that we have ever known individually and collectively.

Know all the spheres and kingdoms of all the Masters are abiding over us, as we entertain Highest Truths for ourselves and all of being. We are open so that God's Light of Wisdom may permeate our being and may accelerate each of us past any and all barriers to fullest incorporation and immediate and direct implementation of the Truth of our Immortal lives now.

And we have many blessings from far to near, from all the Masters, angels and archangels, avatars and all beings of Light, who are with us in Spirit. Centered in the Heavenly Truth, together we hear the Divine Sound of the Universe, the music of the spheres, as we sing the song of the Eternal Soul.

Let us praise all representatives of the Great Wisdom Teachings who have gone before, and evinced beyond a shadow of doubt the Truth of Immortal Life. We are most honored by their eternal Presence, guiding, guarding all of humanity, upholding the beacon of Divine Light throughout the ages. I know we have all been working so long - the leaders, the groups; individually, collectively. We have been working, working, working ~ etching away at all that is false to reveal that ultimate beauty and that glory beyond description within. We have been carrying the torch of Truth, each one of us in our own unique way, working to elevate humanity and ourselves. How Godly! How magnificent that now we have come together to join with each other on the High Plane of Universal Equality, Empathy and Love… that we are consciously establishing the Universal ground and the etheric field for Divine Grace to flow in limitless measure through ourselves and throughout all humanity.

We are honored. We are grateful. God is grateful that we are together. The Heavens are rejoicing right now, I know. The time of Divine Grace and complete emancipation has come.

So I'd like to begin this section with a profound statement by Aurobindo for your deepest consideration. He says, "Since the Divine is fully involved in its creation, man/woman could only be a transitional being ~ not the culmination of evolution."

Thus, this means to us that we are in movement continuously ~ never-ending, now and forever ~ to achieve greater levels of understanding of who and what we really are in God. We are continuously propelled by the Divine, seeking to express its unmatched Attributes ~ its fullest nature -~in, through and as us.

Aurobindo goes on to say, "There is always a continuing transformation or transmutation of the lower or matter-bound nature into the transcendent life more Divine." Thus, realize that as we unify more and more with the central Godhood of our being, the more risen we become. In choosing to always move towards a more all-inclusive consciousness, and incorporation of the Supreme Divine Nature, we accelerate on the ascending cycle ~ our path now straight up to the Central Source and Force of all being and illumination. Through the continuous effort of widening our consciousness, we can come to know greater and greater levels of Reality for ourselves.

Realize: ~ every single one of us, and every single being on this planet is God's perfect intelligent life, becoming more and more conscious of itself. So foremost, before we can begin any type of quantum leaping, we must get deep in our consciousness a new and irrevocable idea of ourselves as one with the total Godhood and no less, for in our minds, most have lived in separation from that Godhood, to greater or lesser degrees.

Every time we have a negative thought about ourselves, a negative idea about anybody else, or what life is, that means we have stepped into a thought of separation from the Great Reality. And, until we unify so completely that we can know no other Truth, we cannot access this Great Reality and all the gifts and blessings that it holds for us.

Try to realize that every one of us comprises the one body ~ God's body, the Divine Manifestation. A *Universal Body Perfect* of the *One Perfect One*. No matter who we are, where we have come from, what we have been through, nevertheless, each one of us right now is eternally one with the Great Cause, the One Cause and animating power of all that lives and moves and has life. And now, through your decision, you can move to a higher state of expression than ever before on the continuum of life.

With all our collective evolution and discoveries, what is the next seal of our Godhood for us to open up and incorporate in all our knowing and attitudes now? What is the single raising factor of greatest import to each, that which can totally transform and uplift all of experience? What do we want to bring out of our quantum and transcendent essence now, in dynamic reality, revealing the ultimate Principle of Life in, through and as our beingness? It is none other than the precious jewel, the most sacred jewel of our Immortality. This recognition is far more than just the acknowledgment of Truth and is not just blindly agreeing, "Oh yeah, I know I'm Immortal." We have come that far as a collective to say: "Yeah, I am Immortal. After I die, my spirit," etc., etc. But I am not talking about futurizing in that way, for this would be to deny the living Truth now. Yet, I am talking about bringing Heaven to earth and living the consciousness of our Immortality now in everything that we do, say and be that we may access the Greater Kingdom of lustrous living right here on Earth. For there is no transformation without inspiration. And there is no evolution without a greater vision to go before you... Something greater about yourself than you have never conceived of before. And this becomes the leading goal and path in mind. Once you have declared what you want to receive, the Divine Mind responds and opens the doors and the ways for you to achieve that.

If we realize we are one with God in the here and now, and we are not living in duality anymore, then we must acknowledge, at least start to mentally acknowledge, that even though one cannot feel it, or understand it as yet, it doesn't matter. So long as you begin the process of daily acknowledging Truth, realizing: "If I am one with God, then I must be one with that Immortal Life of Spirit right here and right now", the doors of untold majesty shall gradually open unto each, as to the great import of this Truth, and all that it means for you.

Your very core values will begin to change, with aspirations reaching up towards the attainment of far greater and more meritorious Spiritual Goals.

Knowing you are one with God, you will know you are connected to the greatest reservoir of blessings for your life.

Realize: "In, through and as every aspect of my being, my physical body, my emotional body, my spiritual body ~ all that I am and all that I need to raise up those Immortal Genes from their slumber to do their work… is to recognize that this is a fact."

Remember, even though we may not be able to accomplish it, even though it may take us an instant or what seems to be a very long time ~ so long as we embrace now the fact that we are "Immortal", we have a strong standpoint to begin, and from which to launch to better worlds. Once established, then we can begin the very important process of etching away all that negativity and all that stuff that encumbers us and bogs us down and prevents us from shining the True Light and Victory and Power that we are as sons and daughters of the Most High.

Understand Divine Potential ~ that golden atom of your Soul that can evolve and evolve eternally unto Light. Let us strive to be the great mystics and avatars of the current age, right here and now. Our job is to do what we can to bring out the imperishable substance of the Divine Body from within, and let it radiate near and far. Let it shine for all to see. Bring out that Christed, perfected body already given to us ~ already within ourselves… Glorious, perfect, and sublime.

Indeed, each can be the fulfillment of the ages right now, if he or she chooses to be…forever becoming more.

The Divine Pattern and blueprint that began with Christ may now come forth. He shot across the face of our earth, like a glowing shaft of light, blessing, renewing and uplifting everyone he touched. The pattern that Jesus laid out through his demonstration of Perfect Principle in and through his very own life is the most ultra-model for all to follow. And, haven't we all have had our crucifixions, along with our daily resurrections? We know what that is, when life springs so bountifully anew around us. We just need to take that one step forward to realize the Divine Life that all are, consciously incorporating those concepts, only taking to our heart, to our being, concepts that reflect the totality of Infinite life.

Yes ~ the time has come where, under Divine Grace, it has become possible for every son and daughter of the Most High to live and directly implement the sublime power and the stellar attributes of risen life, activating the substance of God immediately and directly in our lives... To accelerate and transcend, eliminate and cast off countless eons of the round of death, dying, disease, aging, failure; to at last cure those beliefs in separation, where we have constantly relinquished ourselves to the false gods of death and limitation...to rise free and anew, in every aspect of our lives. It is time now to rise in the universal, depthless body triumphant together - the glory of the Divine Plan made manifest.

When we look at our history, both personal and collective, you can readily see how far we have come ~ and in terms of mass consciousness movement, you can overview the eternal process and witness the ascending cycle of evolution. We see that we have made a tremendous collective effort to express that call to physical perfection that we feel, and that we know that we are. That is the Divine Spark within each and every one, telling us what we really are; that voice of Truth within us, that voice of our Limitless Life is always compelling, prodding us to ascend.

Thus far, we have answered the call through perfecting diet, making all kinds of advancements in medicine, spiritual technology and other methodologies, from the use of the laser to explorations in space. Through it all, we are gaining more and more freedom, stretching our capacities on every front. It is really wonderful.

But still, still there is that silent pressure to do more. And all these efforts towards greater and greater expansion have really been speaking to us of a more sublime phase of life that is ready for us now to occupy where we may rise above the make-dos and the make-overs and even the cosmetic efforts.

And when I say cosmetic, I mean trying to resolve our issues through outer technologies. For at best, external methods can only suffice for a while. And it cannot be that total freedom shall be gained, until we come up to the level of that which is permanent and realize that that force that we are trying to create on the outer actually is a fountain, a spring of life that can be tapped and that exists from within. The quantum leaps and measures of true Divine Progress that shall be gained in the effort of recovering understanding of our true Divine Natures shall defy imagination.

Thus, strive to bring the lustrous Truth out from within your very soul. And then you shall have the understanding that does not fail. You have the talent of re-creation, and can newly create your worlds, once you understand how, and this Gift of Eternal Renewal is already in your life now. Once you have a handle on the Divine Way of manifesting and overcoming, you have then the gift to recreate, and do it again and again. So there is a greater wisdom for each to attain now. And we want to enter into that Immortal Kingdom of direct access with nothing in between ~ to always have direct access through risen recognition of the Greater within, and use of the manifold Divine Gifts which we already possess.

Indeed, each is the most perfect instrument of the Divine ~ a perfect reflection of the great cosmology... the microcosm in the macrocosm. All that the universe is we are in our very structure. All the gifts and talents of self-regeneration, self-renewal, self-healing we already have. And now, through right acknowledgement and understanding, we can bring them out and use them in our moments of challenges and see that they work, delighting to know once again that indeed we have strength, and we do have power. And we may become the Grace Body, the Light Body, the Golden Body, the Body Transcendent and Divine that the great avatars and the mystics always become…as evolution moves us into greater and greater awareness of ourselves.

Now, God has taken us off linear time and placed us on a different cycle. Now, when you think of time, you will almost become unaware of it, and find it no troubling factor at all, for you will know that you are one with timeless being, living and thriving in the Eternal Present, the Eternal Now. There will be no time when the True You is not all there, all capable. I find that the clearer my consciousness gets, the less and less aware of the factor of time I am. It is like time is my friend. I am always on time, in tune with the factor of time. I can operate within time, but there is no sense of plodding or restriction or of anything running me. Moving up in consciousness to embrace the timeless, spaceless state of being is a part of our total elevation.

As you move up beyond linear concepts of time and space, realize time was meant to serve man, and not to bind. Now, instead of thinking of yourself in terms of birth, then proceeding to walk a linear time line ~ now it is one o'clock, now it is two o'clock, then it's Thursday, then it's Friday, then I do this, then I do that, and so it goes, careening toward the inevitable, ultimate death…you will think of yourself as moving ever upwards, in never-ending spirals of Light. How sad it is when persons live the precious gift of life against this inevitable, ultimate death ~ with all of one's efforts going toward preventing the perceived "inevitable". What a strain on the great life force which proceeds so freely on its own when it is unencumbered. Often, I will give only "one long day" to events and cycles that appear to take years to complete, claiming no toll at all.

Realize that living on the "Ascending Cycle" doesn't mean you are leaving the planet, yet the "Ascension" is the ascending cycle within that transforms the body within into that Golden Body. And every time there is a new understanding, there is immediate and all-encompassing transformation. There is new activity in the body. There is greater light. There is greater beauty. There is greater radiance made manifest, and on some level, everyone knows the benefits from living on the spiral of Light, on the wings of elevated Higher Thought and expectation.

You've seen friends on a good day, and you might immediately comment, "Gee! You look ten years younger, like you took ten years off your life." What happened to them? They probably had a good thought. That is how powerful a thought is! Though a negative thought may have persisted for eons of time, one constructive thought has immediate transformative power.

Imagine if your thought ascends to affirm, "I am one with God." Imagine how much can drop away from you then. In order to ascend beyond issues of the past, realize the process requires greater and greater consciousness, which then produces illumination, which in turn produces Light, which then produces transformation.

197

Ask yourself: "Well, if I am not careening toward death, then what am I doing?" Get a new vision for yourself. Affirm: "My life is a God story ~ I am ever increasing Light. Every single day, I am more and more Light. I am more and more the radiant life of God. I am more and more understanding. I am more and more the living incorporation and manifestation of Divine Principles of wholeness, power and peace. I am on an endless, never-ending cycle of better and better every day." There are no finalities in God. Let us forget that already. We keep thinking in terms of terminals, finality. "It's over. That is it." Yet, that is not a Truth. Immortality is not up for us to decide about. It is a life principle. It is a self-existent Principle of Life, which we have, and we are either going to rejoice in it and use it and bring it out whenever and wherever we can or we are going to continue to deny the Great Reality, in as much saying, "No. God did not give birth to the planets and to all that is and to myself."

That is the nature of separation thought, feeling "I am apart somehow". Thus, one now knows one's self as an ever increasing light moving upward in greater and greater understanding. And, how do we move up? We must choose. Nothing happens without our choice, without our conscious recognition. For we are manifest as beings of free will. We have choice to believe in what we want to believe in, and choice to aspire toward what we want to create, with the power of Divine Will to support. And we can choose the Higher Path right now in this great moment of momentous evolution, where everything is possible to each and every one. We can choose to give up, once and for all and forever, the lesser for the greater. Or we can choose, once again, to do the old thing ~ close the door on the mind, stay in our own limitation thoughts, and close the door to the great pearls and gems of wisdom and life and bounty that lay before us.

I know that there are no accidents and that each who has chosen to read this book already knows he or she is the Immortal Light of God, and has materialized this opportunity to dwell in Highest Thought. It is the choice of your Highest Self. You indeed have manifest yourself in this circumstance. Your consciousness did that, materializing right and perfect opportunity to imbibe, now, in the renewing elixir of your own truth and your burgeoning greater freedom ~ that portion, which has been held away for so long. Now, as we rise freer, one of the main changes that occurs on the emotional plane is that we get to a place where we come off the victim consciousness ~ where everyone else is to blame. "Oh, they are doing it 'to' me. Oh, I can't help it. Oh, I can't." This level of thinking is loaded with lots of self-negative language which denies the ability of the Godhood within.

And I am not saying that we should not recognize a temporary state of mind, i.e. "I am not feeling so good today," but we must come to a place where we can say, "I know there is that within me that can overcome this whatever." And that takes us to the next level, where blame and shame no longer exist. At this level, we know, then, that consciousness is all and rules earth or our experience. Heaven (consciousness) rules earth, our experience. And, through our consciousness, through the thoughts we are thinking and the visions we are projecting, just like the camera, we are projecting the substance of our inner thought out into the subtle substance of experience, the outer form of the inner mental/emotional experience that we are having. Thus it is that consciousness produces experience in the eternal sequence of Cause/Effect. Experience has no power whatsoever of its own.

This is very important to understand, in order to really avoid always thinking something other than ourselves has the power. God said, "I have given you dominion over the earth, lands and the seas, and all that is." What do you think that really means? Realize, each of us has total authority over all things of our physical, mental, emotional and spiritual worlds. Thus, we want to claim our authority and stop blaming and realize there is something in us that we can tap, we can call upon, and it shall go forth and do the thing for us in most exquisite harmony and perfection, once we have asked.

We must ask for what we want, choosing to engage the Higher Wisdom and Power in our every aspiration, knowing we are beings of free will, knowing that this perfect life force which we call God, Great Creator, "I Am that I Am" of the many Divine names…is ever at hand. We are not talking person here, yet referencing the Great Source of all existence, beyond person, but infinitely personal to all. We are talking about that great life force that manifests all of life. We know this perfect life force of God streams through us. The body is like an electrical pole, and according to our awareness and our acceptance, that is how much of that great power and life force can stream through you, an individual point of grounding of the Infinite and the Eternal in the matter plane.

Ever rejoice that the perfect life force of God streams through you and all. Realize this Divine Force lives in you, the very flame of life at the central point of your being. It is a force capable of doing of itself independently and infinitely whatever we have in mind without exception. How can we say, "I can't?" Reflect upon this wondrous statement ~ "Our Father is a father of the living and not the dying." Father of 100 percent total Limitless Life Principle knowing no death, no power in death, no power in disease, no power in aging. These are not a thing to the infinite and the sublime in you, and not a power. These are not a cause to life, even though we go on getting ill and doing the things we are doing, not because we are really choosing it, but as a result of the immense amount of programming that the human being endures. It is like walking around hit on the head...in a state of fog and delusion, the great Maya, as it were.

And, now, thankfully we are waking up from all of this programming and the accompanying negatives, that each comes into in particular ways, when we come into this life. Know you are the embodiment of 100 percent perfect Life Principle. And as we etch away at these notions that we don't need anymore, and that never really belonged to us, we go Higher and Higher in awareness, stretching far into the Heavens, and life around us begins to show forth the hidden bounty that was always there.

Did you ever hear somebody say, "There is not enough?" Realize that is merely a thought going around. It is not a thing of itself, but it will become a thing as soon as you give it acceptance. Now, in the greater awareness, one can rise above, claiming an Abundant Principle that never changes or runs out…of Infinite Ways and Means. Stop accepting what you don't want to experience. Stop expecting that invincible God-in-you, is vulnerable to any passing influence. Affirm, "That has nothing to do with me. There is only Divine Abundance going around in Perfection, plenty and to spare."

This is so important to grasp, if you can understand… how the purity of consciousness is so broken up by negative programming. We are so conditioned to think, "I'm going to live so long. Then I'm going to put my body in a box." And some of us think: "It is going to be over then", and some of us think, "Well, then I'll go on as a spiritual body." Or, "I am going to attain Heaven after I get into the box." Yet, realize, as a great Yogi friend of mine said, "If you don't reach illumination before you go in the box, you are not getting it after."

Be infinitely grateful for all the opportunities for growth that earth experience provides. Realize the place for illumination, the

Heaven of Highest Mind, and achieving that most exalted state of bliss …is here and now. The place for unification is here and now on the great planet Earth, where you can bring God's life into your daily life, your daily thought patterns and all that you are about, building the Golden Spiritual Body within.

Our Father of Life, the great cosmic Mother/Father, hasn't got a clue what we are talking about when we say there is death, lack and illness going around. But we are free to play that out until we decide to get off it.

This is a strong and illuminating question that you can really contemplate and consider in your quiet, meditative times. If you acknowledge, "There is only life," to yourself, and that life is omnipotent life, God's life, ask yourself can there be any validity to "I have to put up with this physical condition," or whatever trouble or challenging condition you may be facing? This is very important because you are changing your point of identity, at the root and causal level. And it is what you identify with at the root of your being that compels or causes the creation that you experience. What you believe to be true about yourself causes your experience.

Passing thoughts really don't change anything about the Truth about you, not a hair on your head. In other words, you will always be Immortal because you were established that way. But, if you do not accept it, you will not be able to bring out that greatness in the here and now. You still have the freedom to die and get up and try it all over again: "Maybe I'll get it better next time." Yet, isn't it better to start your transcendence now, with all the rich opportunities hidden in the challenges that life brings? *Learn to rely on Infinite Principle and Law. When you feel you "can't", learn to depend on the Greater Capacity for your every transcendent victory*

Do we know the tremendous biological fact that everyone, biologically and scientifically, is the exact same age? This is such a tremendous insight that when I read the scientific report, it really just hit me, and it just affirmed more deeply what I already know. Do you know that you are biologically the same age as everyone else? How old is that? At the most, one year. Biologically, with the constant movement of cells and the constant restoration that automatically goes on within your body, all are only one year maximum in biological age ~ three months, most likely ~ and I say every moment, for we are the ever-renewing life of Spirit.

To know this Truth is to truly understand the magnificence and flexibility of your physical life, though your consciousness may have experienced more or less of what we call time. This true understanding gives us a far richer dimension of understanding, opening the possibility of living in this realization of constant opportunity to re-charge, restore and renew. Biologically each is the same age as he or she was at one year old. So this really gives pause to think about, "Well, if this is the truth, then what am I doing? Why am I aging? Why am I getting sick? What am I buying into there?" You see? Nothing can work in your life, nothing can become operational until you agree to give it power. But the Truth is, the mother is the same age as the child. There is no old and young in Spirit. There is only Infinite Ever-Present life doing the thing it knows to do, which is to perpetuate itself.

Thus it is only our limited and negative ideas that have stopped this great power that we own from doing the thing it can do. The intelligence within us knows how to constantly regenerate us every single moment if we know how to let go, if we know how to engage it, to let this wondrous reality be… if we know how to praise and give reverence to this tremendous life force.

Understand that truly the body is a Temple of God. We have heard this, but to understand this awesome Truth from the depth of it ~ when we say that body is the pure life of God, we must know it cannot be anything other. It cannot be. For there is only one cause to all of life which is perfect. Any artist is compelled to paint from his or her own vision of itself. You always see the distinct handiwork present. And so it is with the Father. The Divine signature is hidden there in every design. So too, we carry on the work of the great Master artist/architect in our very own lives by manifestation of that very same perfection, which it knows for itself, and that we are singularly endowed with. Do we realize the great Temple of God that we live in? Do we love it? You know of people who say, "Well, yeah, I am a Spiritual being, but that has nothing to do with my body." Now, in enlightened understanding, we know, "There is only Spirit, and matter is just the manifest material expression of Spirit." It is the same thing, like water becomes ice.

Do we love and dwell in our temple in deepest reverence and understanding of its immense capacities? Do we revere the Immortal Treasure we have been given? Do we know this Temple of the Living God is a perfect self- regenerating system of intelligence, light and love that is constantly renewing itself of its own? If you have ever observed the life force working, if you just stood back and watched it working anywhere ~ in nature, for example or felt it in your own body, you would see every Divine Principle in operation before you.

Witness when you get a minor injury or suffer a minor bruise, how sure you are of that mighty self-healing power, as you say, "That's nothing. It'll be taken care of." What do you think it is that takes care of it? What heals up that wound, and then a day later, it's all fine? And you did nothing. You just knew that something was going to take care of it. Within is the natural tendency to heal all.

It is that very same force that would mend worlds, if only we would recognize and allow, that very same force that would mend all without limit, if we would let. Life moves to perpetuate itself, intelligent life, to correct itself, to make the adjustments and to do whatever is necessary for its ongoingness. And we can take advantage of this great and unlimited Power once we have taken all of our blockages out of the way.

Are you willing to put all the past behind you, releasing it that you may rise anew ~ and this is the big thing, the dividing line between minor and major healing, and the only question that counts. The force of the collective mind throughout history has pulled us and magnetized us away from limitless Truth. Just like in the Woody Allen movies ~ if you were standing at the street corner, waiting for the bus, and the minds were opened up next to you, and you heard what was going through those minds, you could see and hear that diverse mental atmosphere that we live in. Now maybe you would be lucky enough to be standing next to a guru, and that would be great. But maybe you are not, and in that case, then you must be your own guru. This is the force of what we call the race mind, the collective mind ~ that collection of negation and varying opinion that is impressing itself upon us all the time.

Truly ask; are you willing to break the bonds of tradition ~ those thought fields and beliefs that are traditional and status quo today? This field of thought has even built up to become a moral issue. That is how fixed a traditional field of thought can be. Could it be immoral to live forever? Just realize how much we have really distorted the life force. So our being willing to let it all go, in favor of Truth, is a great stride to make.

Ask yourself, "Am I willing to break the bonds of tradition and erase my beliefs in tragedy and morbidity, all this guising over the glorious Truth, passing a large cloud over the radiant Presence of God in me?" Am I willing to stand free and step out of being a statistic, and be an individualization of God-Consciousness?" Are we willing to activate our full glory through conscious choice, or shall we say, "Oh, well, sometime, maybe. Not now. Later on, down the line...after this or after that." For the mightiest of changes to come about, it indeed requires the active, conscious engagement of the individual will. All transformation happens solely through conscious choice. You have dominion. All the powers of Conscious choice, coupled with gifts of Divine Decision and Determination are yours to live the God life that you have in all its aspects.

To stand firm in the midst in your Citadel of Truth is the Highest use of your Divine Will possible. You have been given will to be able to activate, through decision, what you want to manifest. It is your determination, your choice whether to rise or to stay at status quo ~ now and in this time. If every single one of us chooses to build a better life ~ to demonstrate that something greater about the Universal Cosmic Life, it would be the greatest boon to our fellow beings, for these Principles are common to everyone everywhere, regardless. And, for those who are brave enough to stand up and say, "I go forth in my evolution, and I'm going to demonstrate this Principle. I choose to."... Well, pretty soon, you will have other people asking, "Well, what are you doing that is working so well?"

And then you will have a multitude of people following and lighting the way for more. So it is up to us who are in the know and who have consciousness to be the embodiment such as Christ, be a living embodiment of the Principles of life, including Immortality. How do we do that? Very simply...always with the consciousness of Love and recognizing the Divine Presence and Power within each and every one, regardless of what condition appears.

Thus, if some friend is ill, we say, "I know there is a power in you that can overcome this." Instead of saying, "Oh, poor you," where you are just getting in there with the one who is suffering, compounding their condition and making more of it, rather than inspiring and freeing the being to know who they are, which is the greatest thing we can do for anyone...now you will be an agent of Divine Freedom, lifting all up, an inspiration and a Light of Hope. So, you see, we can adopt this attitude and generate this light of our knowing everywhere we are, in every instance. It doesn't matter what it is, it only matters that we know and affirm that "Nothing is Impossible to one whose mind is stayed on God." And we are either going to add unto this universe and be a plus in the lives of others, or we are going to restrict the Divine Life Force in ourselves and others, just going around in the same old way.

We want to bless and give thanks, deepest thanks, and recognize and praise our Universal Body of being right now through recognizing its timeless perfection of God's Light and Love.

Wherever you go, you will be in a body. Whether here, there, or in any dimension… You will always manifest some sort form of Light. So you might as well get the Truth of Being down in consciousness…your new and wonderful Foundation that shall never fail you: "My life is one with God's Life. Whatever God is (All the Love, All the Infinite Capacity) I am."

I want to share with you an extraordinary event that happened for me, something so marvelous about this great and transcendent healing power we all have access to every moment and trusting to it. Very typically, when I'm dwelling on a subject, I receive a major demonstration, and at such important times when preparing to speak at an event, often wonderful challenges and opportunities to "walk the talk" come my way. Thus, when preparing for a major event at Carnegie Hall, I was thinking about the subject of Immortality and the ways I have personally used the Divine Power of Light to heal and to mend and the ways it has always served to improve life for me. It was then, that a mighty occurrence took place that profoundly illustrates how we can use directly the Principle, and how there is just no barrier between us and the Great Source, if only we know it.

I had a loft in my New York home, which was six feet off the ground, and, while working on the presentation I would give, I had been in deep meditation during this period. I had never fallen off that loft in 30 plus years, but one night I just got up, and I stepped out into the middle of space. I just got up, while still asleep and walked out! And I landed, no less, in the meditation position! As you can imagine, falling from such a height onto the hard cement floor below was excruciatingly painful, and although there were no visible bruises, my entire body was in agony and I just could not move, nor get up. And, this was only two and a half weeks before a major talk on Immortality that I was to give at Carnegie Hall.

With just two and a half weeks to go I had my six-foot drop to earth. I was the yogi that fell to earth ~ and so after asking my assistant to help me, screaming and pleading, "Please! I can't walk! I can't walk!"…with his help, I got myself to the couch, and finally, once I was in a position where I was laying down and off my feet ~ I discovered that actually, there was not one bruise. Much to my relief, nothing on the body was affected with the exception of my right leg and hip.

A friend said to me, "Oh, you know, the right leg is your future." So I said, "Well, at least I landed on the right one!"

So now, this was very painful. Yet, I remained grateful that I didn't have a bruise ~ not one. There was not one bruise and nothing apparently broken, though it seemed that my back could possibly be injured for life. And I knew instantly, even in the midst of the horrible pain, that I was in charge of how this situation would turn out, reminding myself of how important it was to remain in Truth.

211

Thus I began the process out of misery into the discovery of the power of the Infinite Light of Healing in me, as I unequivocally stated to myself: "OK, Linda. Your consciousness is going to direct how this turns out. And there is no way, Reverend Dr. Linda, that you are going to go to Carnegie Hall in a wheelchair or on crutches. That is unacceptable to me."

I realized the Divine was giving me a sudden and unanticipated challenge to prove my point of the Perfect Healing Power. There were other mysteries, too, that revealed themselves to me, as the healing unfolded. But here is the major thing to understand. What I have learned to do whenever I am in a critical situation now, is I immediately move in consciousness to hold up the pattern of what I know to be true about God ~ God's life, the Divine Life of the Creator Mind. And I say to myself, "If it is not true for the Creator, it is not true for me." "If it is not true for God, it is not true for me."

And so, with that bold statement, I indeed set the course of what would become my demonstration. You see? Even in the midst of the most tormenting pain, it was my decision to either succumb to the apparency or to center in the profound Healing Light, and I decided this event was going to turn out right, and somehow I would be perfectly healed, and moreover in two and a half weeks' time. And, with that profound decision, everything I needed to assist me to rise up and overcome came forth.

As I lay there in utter shock in the middle of the night, completely immobilized, I began to inspect and test the severity of my condition, and I found that with concerted effort, I could still do all kinds of yoga postures from a prone position. I could even stand up, if I was very careful, and I could feel my toes and even bend my knees a little bit to assist myself to try and stand. But I could not place pressure, not an ounce, on that right leg, as the trauma to the muscles and bone was so great. So I knew I had to fix this quick. And here are some of the transcendent tools I used and some of the wondrous occurrences that happened for me. As I lay there in pain, yet still centered in Truth, first I got a vision that the pain I was experiencing was not true for God-in-me, thus God-in-me cannot have muscle problems, nor suffer injury to any bones whatsoever. "God cannot be traumatized, so neither can I." And I proceeded in this fashion and meditated very deeply. And I then asked myself, "OK, what is my body? What is it really? What is this leg here?" And, my answer was: "My leg is the light of God in fact, form and function, meant to give me freedom of movement and support."

Now, when light falls to earth, does anything offend, does anything happen? Are there any wounds? Anything broken? Any traumas? None of these things occur. Descending Light would just rest gently on earth, though I will have to improve my landing, I'll admit. But I was beginning to realize, "Yes. My leg is light. My body is light." Not only that, I started to say, "God, I want to be on that foot in three days and no less." OK?

So I started meditating more deeply day and night, seeing the light, acknowledging, praising my leg, praising its strength, its invincibility, thanking my leg for always being so supportive of me, giving it Gratitude for carrying me around so wonderfully, as I climbed all the mountains I had climbed and enjoyed great flexibility all my life. I praised, blessed and streamed Light and Breath over, in, around and through into the areas that seemed to hurt the most, feeling them relaxing, feeling all straighten out. In the meantime, I was telling the Greater Principle, which we call God ~ I said, "God, tomorrow I want to walk. Tomorrow, I want everything that is out of joint put back in place." And so, in this way, I worked my way back to perfection. And then I thought, "Not only do I want all of this back in perfection, I want it greater than it was ever before. If I had to fall to earth, it has got to be for a good reason, and that means maybe I'll be able to get rid of that little glitch I had since youth in my spine." And perhaps this was another constructive purpose for this event. I was not going to entertain any negative outcome whatsoever, only Giving Thanks that the greater would come forth.

I envisioned myself in not only a condition of health and well-being, with great mobility, pain free, but ultimately arriving at a state of greater physical ease than ever before… through recognizing "I am one with God, and with God all things are possible."

Indeed, all things are possible, including instantaneous healing, but you must have the consciousness of it, or these powers

214

have no place to operate. You must call upon it. By the time I got to Carnegie Hall, I was perfectly fine, and I had never felt better, and I do believe I probably got just the minor little adjustment that I needed in my spine. By my word and faithful envisioning it became so.

As I realized more and more that my body is Light, healing rapidly progressed, and regardless of the programming that the body is composed of muscles and it is dense and can suffer irreparable injury, and you can break bones and you can do this and that, I wasn't going to buy into that. I affirmed, "It is perfect light and intelligence. Whatever has gone on with it, it knows how to repair itself, and I am stepping out of the way and letting the all capable and all readjusting Divine Intelligence in me do it."

My students and friends of the time witnessed a fast transition through this stage, and this is how it was accomplished. Regardless of any human tendency to get into grief and fear, I overrode all, staying with the Principle, and thanking God in advance for my perfect healing too. Now the other thing I realized, and this is very powerful in any type of healing, is that there is that Immortal Essence of Light and Intelligence always resident within us all, and because I made a passageway and because I was open to receive ~ and not only that, I insisted on it ~ this unassailable knowing and Faith is the very force that brought it forth for me. It was such a very powerful manifestation for me.

215

The other key factor to realize, and this is true in any challenge that you have, is to understand that when a challenge comes to you, it has come to deliver you a message. And, when you receive the message, the messenger can disappear. And that was another aspect I worked on. I asked, "What was the purpose in this?" And I began to see. The event itself required a lot of preparation, which meant that I needed to stay in one spot to be able to do all the set-up of the hall, all the phone calls that needed to be made, etc. I love to travel. But it was very clear that for the three weeks prior, the Infinite had need of me there in one spot.

So many miracles and wonderful things have happened, as I say, on the way to Carnegie Hall.

But clearly the Infinite had wanted me there and knew how to speak to me, because I do love to go climbing mountains, and that is the way I get my inspiration. But it was another kind of wisdom and inspiration that I was being given. So remember this: When you are in a challenge, look for the meaning, and when you get the message, the messenger (the troublesome condition) can disappear. Look for the gold within, and remember that there is nothing that you cannot heal, that the Divine Power in you cannot heal ~ through Light Consciousness. It is such a tremendous gift.

Even as I lay there still somewhat immobilized, the next evening I awoke somewhere around 2:00AM and the television was

216

still on. Like a messenger from space, the programming that was on was all about legs, and the science of movement from the animal kingdom to the glory of the human being. As I lay there half awake and watching ~ the information was pouring into my subconscious mind, reminding me of how to walk, how to place my feet, and so on. Surely, all of Heaven and earth was filled with richest instruction for me, as this amazing miracle programming just appeared out of the blue for me. Really, I just have never seen anything like it.

I was somewhere about a week and a half into the healing, and I thought, "Well, maybe I'd better have an x-ray." At the first, everyone around me had urged, "Rush to the hospital." Do this, do that. And I said, "I am not doing it. I am just not doing it. It is the middle of the night, and I am just not getting into that. I am giving God time."

And then sometime later, I thought, as I was improving ~ "Well, maybe I should have an x-ray and see if there is a little itsy-bitsy something there." And I called my doctor, because at that point, I still couldn't walk down stairs. And she said, "Oh, I'll come to see you." And I said, "God, if you really are it, then by the time this doctor comes, I want to be so well that she tells me, 'There's nothing wrong with you.'" And as I said that, a whole shaft of light suddenly passed through my whole right side. It was really something.

217

Shortly, the doctor rang the doorbell, and she came in, looked me over, tested a few areas, and then emphatically announced, "You are fine. You are fine. Just stand up." I said, "Oh, sure!" "I don't know if I can… It still hurts." She once again affirmed, "You are fine. Here is a little muscle relaxant. You are fine."

Yet, I wanted to check every detail and be sure she knew what I was experiencing, "Well, doctor, when I bend this way, this happens and that happens." And she said, "You are fine." She was totally fulfilling my treatment, and she wasn't going to hear anything I had to say about that, and she is a very brilliant woman, so I had every good reason to trust her judgment. And so it was that my words went before me, even in spite of my little feelings of doubt.

Some time ago, my mother went through an experience that was more than challenging to say the least. She is generally in great consciousness and, therefore, great health, a very beautiful, wondrous, kind-of very ageless being. And she had a severe stomach condition that happened to her, as a result of some bad medication prescribed that caused her to be hospitalized for five weeks, teetering on the border of life and death. This had really caused fear in my father, as he dealt with the possibility of losing her.

And so, I went home to visit my mother, hoping I could in my way add some constructive energy to this dire situation. Both of my parents were just so normally healthy, and everybody was

218

thrown by this constant state that had been going on for five weeks, and it seemed to be getting worse.

Though she was deathly ill, I meditated upon the Infinite Horizon ~ realizing there is no horizon too great for her to attain in God, and that she could be perfectly well, coming up over this by knowing God had an even greater idea of physical well-being than she had ever dreamed possible or known.

I went immediately to talk to my mother, and I just said, "Mom, just remember there is only one power that heals. No matter what the doctors give you. No matter what they do. There is only one power, and that is the life of God in you."

Now, if I had been thinking of her in terms of age and vulnerability, instead of knowing the limitless Light and Life of God that she truly is...my prayers would have been ineffective. And so I persisted to know that through this circumstance, not only would she recover, she would experience greater health than ever before.

And so it was that indeed she did come out victorious, by the power of the vision for herself, her undaunting Faith in the All-in-the-All, and by streamlining out of her life certain activities that had been sapping her strength. After five weeks of vomiting ~ the very next morning, there was no more vomiting. She was put back on light food, and she was out of the hospital on Sunday ~ in two days.

Overjoyed and so relieved, she said, "It's a miracle. It's a miracle." And I said, "No, mom. You are the miracle. Your Faith has made you whole." Once again, it was her consciousness and Faith in the Greater that healed. She only needed to be reminded of the Perfect Truth.

And then when I treated/prayed for her, I treated that the experience would lead her even into greater health than she has ever known, and I took time to visualize that blessing possibility, to the point where there was no more doubt in me. And now she is unstoppable.

Now she knows the secret of consciousness, and the ever-present Infinite Capacity upon which she can rely.

And so, when I recently called her to wish her a Happy Birthday, she said; "Don't wish me that. I am not into counting those days and years anymore." As she continued on, she gleefully announced: "I am reversing the aging process. I am looking younger and younger every day." And it is true, and still more than true to this day.

Realize how this wisdom of knowing the power of consciousness can save us. This knowing can set us on the right path and get us those glories, those miracles, those joys of our life that we deserve.

Truly, at the point of seeming death, we are in fact at the point of Infinite possibility for greater life and complete resurrection, if only we keep our minds on the power of God within, and strive to contemplate the greater Divine Pattern of overcoming.

Realize in any "traumatic" situation ~ You are that Light cannot be damaged. Though muscles and bones, etc. may seem dense and hard to heal, it is never the case. Just let any trauma pass right through you, and go on its way.

Then there is the issue of weight. Know ~ "I don't have weight. If I am light, I don't have weight. All are the same weight, for all are Light. We are always Light, and we are all the qualities of Light. Affirm: "If I have no weight, if I am light, I cannot be traumatized", and so on and so on. Take yourself to the regal place of surety in every matter. Once you conceive of body as flowing cells of Infinite Light, flexible with lots of God space in between, completely responsive to your thoughts about it, you will understand how easy it is to heal. Draw Divine Conclusions about yourself. "I am one with Perfect Intelligence, and it knows how to repair a leg, realign bones, as well as heal a little cut finger, and just as easily too.

If it used to be thought of as God's punishment ~ for the erring consciousness ~ to die at 900 years, how have we shortened our very own lives, and what can we do to improve? And if this is God's punishment for loss of consciousness about the Truth, what must be the extent of God's Grace and Love for us, once awareness is recovered, even to the least degree?

When a child comes in, a child is fresh from the cosmos, and it knows who it is. And then immediately, it catches the thought field that it comes into. As prevailing thought of particular environment, tradition, and cultural mores come in, the heavenly light suddenly gets caught up in the mesmerism and morbidity of the negative thoughts of the ones around him or her, who immediately start to advise the limitless being of the inevitability of their death.

That is a horror story of horror stories. What this does to this beautiful and pure Infinite being is build up these shadows of futility, sadness and despair. Here you have a being coming into this plane with highest aspiration and hopes, filled with the glory of Divine Life and Love and awareness of the Divine Birth-Right to express that which he or she is to the Highest and Best.

And now that same glory of God begins to build an ultimate failure consciousness. Those limiting notions begin to seep in and underlie every activity, no matter how great the accomplishment.

In this way, we have become very drugged by all these notions of limitation and conflict abounding. Then we take it for real, but it isn't and never was the Great Reality, rich in limitless possibilities…and no matter where we are, or what has transpired, we will always be provided with infinite opportunity to work this very great understanding that we are talking about, to recover the Kingdom of our original natures, to consciously shed untruth.

In this fervent hope, let us not lose anymore our precious line of connection with the Infinite Creative Spirit and Joy of our True selves. Let us awaken our Divine Will to stand up for Immortal life and Love for every being... for our rights in God. We are the heirs to the Kingdom, and we know that our determination to rise and to express as something greater shall be the yeast that raises the dough.

And if you decide to live and enjoy utmost Truth, with all the force of your being ~ is there anything that can be done to you to sway you off your path? No, there isn't...for all authority of choice is yours.

If you've made a wishy-washy decision, chances aren't too good. But if you make a decision with all the force of your being, you can go as far as you want to go. Never stop 'til you are the totality of God-Consciousness.

Try me, and I will prove you true! Use every opportunity that comes your way to realize greater and greater Truth. Remember the words of the sublime Christ: *"I have come that you may overcome the world". "The Father is within". He who looks upon me sees the Father!"... that great Force of Life within.*

Often, center in Truth and do your meditative exercises. Such frequent practice will help you to ground the material that we have been talking about, causing inner realization to take place.

And, to give power to your contemplations, the following reveals the greatest secret that we can ever know.

This is the one great secret of all the mystics, the avatars, the yogis, the alchemists ~ all have realized this one great thing…the transcendent power of Unity. All of the great mystery teachings that are now available to us in our everyday life are about bringing Heaven to Earth. All illumine the Power of bringing our Highest Consciousness into our everyday experience ~ incorporating it and embodying it. It is no longer, "Well, sometime I will get into Truth. Maybe next time around I will try it." The entire study of Immortal Truth is really about bringing Heaven to Earth in the here and now.

In ancient alchemy, the secret of the philosopher's stone is continuously referenced and sought. This profoundly magical stone represents the quintessential element, revered by all. And what is this stone? What does this stone represent but the purest consciousness of the Oneness, the very *Oneness of All That Is*. Every mystic has realized this. Every great being has realized this one fundamental fact ~ that the one Supreme Substance, the one and only substance of life is *Divine Light and Love* animating all of consciousness. All of conscious life, from the most refined to the most densified matter levels is the embodiment and the essence is Light and Love. In the realization of the Unity of All ~ comes a noble synthesis of every atom of the universe.

Therefore, the great understanding is that there is only one thing that is manifest in multiple manifestations and varieties of forms, and the many unique manifestations, like the rainbow of beautiful faces and cultures across the sea of humanity. All are like singular radiances on the face of a crystal. Yet, all are unified at the center, and all contain that crystal center of all Divine Substance.

Therefore, this great understanding that there is only one power, one life, one force, one absolute substance that forms the Great Reality; and the knowing that we are it, and we live in it, and we breathe it, and we partake of it, and it is our life, is the much sought-after understanding of the philosopher's stone. Here base metal may be turned to gold by adding the right element of thought. And from this understanding, we can begin to create any and all transformations that we desire.

All methods of truest and highest maintenance of life in all its forms arise and are directly connected to the application of this Immortal Truth; "There is Only One." Understanding that we may use the indestructible essence, the quintessential elixir of life, as they say in alchemy, this fount of incomprehensible light, love, breath and will for whatever means and purposes is key to liberty of every kind... transcendent, ultimately and absolutely of every condition. Thus, build up your force from within, and whenever you undergo treatment, know and declare that the Divine Healing Power is at work, through all avenues, and always affirm complete success from the beginning, never entertaining anything less than perfect Divine Outcome; i.e., "Divine Intelligence works through the surgeon, performing the perfect operation. Every aspect is surrounded by Divine Love."

But we should know that we can aspire even to go greater than here... that there is that within us that can, of its own. And, it is important to try to release, as we can, as it is comfortable, any and all dependencies on systems and forms, and try to work direct with the Divine within us, according to our own pace and rhythm.

Thus, in raising what is called the Golden Body or the Light Body within, what are our methods of direct alchemy and transformation? Remember when Jesus said to the disciples, "Come follow me.", and they went up to the top of the mountain, and for that stunning moment, he just let them see his radiant Light Body.

For the disciples, that was the pinnacle moment of transfiguration, where they got to see their beloved leader in his true form. For a moment, he dropped the physical and let them see the ultra-Divine Reality of our being, an atomic field of Light. In all instances, we want to acknowledge the Presence of the Divine Force.

And then, just as quickly, he returned to his ordinary state, and together they came down the mountain again. But, for that heightened moment, Jesus let them know the inner truth of the radiant light of our being, silently, secretly animating all ~ First Cause behind all.

So to raise this light body in ourselves now, first and foremost, we already have one of the greatest tools of ascension, and that is the capacity to forgive. Forgiveness cleanses and prepares the emotional body. And we all have multi-levels that we are operating on ~ our mental bodies, our emotional bodies, our physical bodies, our Spiritual bodies...and we are responsible for the well-being of that team, through the way that we are thinking and feeling, and the beliefs that we hold true.

Through forgiveness, we cleanse and prepare our emotional body from that density of angers and hates and fears that make us ill, make us live short lives, and drag us down. Now, we begin to practice to monitor our emotions and to choose to change them to absolute joy and love, knowing joy and love is the natural way unencumbered Spirit expresses itself. Practicing living in the consciousness of purest joy of unassailable Faith and Love, regardless of what appears...causes Light to increase throughout.

Whenever the glory of Truth is contemplated, doesn't it cause a great broad smile of contentment to appear? Whenever you are around those who are risen, aren't you uplifted by the serene and joyous atmosphere that seems to surround? Realize, the joyous individual is not laughing for nothing. Joy springs from deep within. He or she is laughing because they know that they know that they know that they know the lustrous Immortal Truth of being. Thus, on the mental plane, healing any ideas of separation, duality or opposition to anyone or anything in life is also good for the emotional body, as emotions correspond to the quality of thought.

Life cannot oppose itself and never denies itself. It is compelled to express the richness of Infinite Life and wonder that it is. You want to be one in all your ways with the true nature of the Life Force itself. All the ideas persons have been raised with ~ that someone or something is opposing us, or that we are separate from a certain group of people, a particular nation, religion or culture act to deflate spirit, and lessen access to the mighty current of Divine Love and Unity that sustains the whole universe.

There are so many thought patterns that have caused us to live in a divided mind about who we are in essence, as one with all of life. And these must be healed, because to the degree that we feel separate from anyone, anything ~ regardless of how real or justifiable it may seem, such thoughts will only act to hurt and limit ourselves. There is no reason, and there is no good excuse not to find a point of oneness with everyone and everything. To the degree that you are feeling separate, acting separate, behaving separate, you

228

cannot access the Kingdom. Thus, each must perform the alchemy of changing separation and duality thoughts and feelings into unity. The emotions must be healed and liberated, freed to be a great constructive force, for they are meant to be our great creative fire and fuel.

Emotions are the actual fuel that empowers thought to manifest. What I feel strongly about, what I feel deeply about ~ not just what I think, but what I truly feel deeply about… I will manifest by the Law, and when my feelings get behind something, the whole force of God's life is charged-up there. I become a mighty attracting and manifesting force. Now, you may not want to have dinner with a person, but you must strive to realize God's life there, no matter how little of the Light may be showing forth.

Thus, realize the ultimate value of your emotional life. Originally the feelings were known as a manifesting instrument. And so in the metaphysical world, we practice thinking only the Highest and the Best that can be conceived. When we think in terms of creating anything, whether it be a job, a partner, illumination ~ no matter what it is, we immediately start to picture the thing that we desire, giving inner form to it by dwelling upon it with the greatest love, joy, harmony, peace, sense of flowingness and affinity. Once the optimum picture has arisen from our Divine Self, we give thanks for that, knowing that the things that we desire in our lives will be drawn to us most harmoniously in this manner… And that we will project to all of life these qualities of Spirit, of love and enthusiasm and goodness and desire for everyone's well-being, because we know what goes around comes around. Instantly the content of our thought and expectation comes around, and, so too, what we pass around to others comes back to us, on the Infinite Circle of Being.

Thus, we want to cure our emotions through utilizing the sacred tool of Forgiveness, realizing that as we do that, and as we free our emotional bodies, the Divine and Creative Law is free to do the thing more greatly, more instantaneously for us... that it was always meant to do, and that is to be the creative force powering our thoughts into glorious form. But to the degree that the emotions are stuck, they cannot act in support of the new. They must hide away, powerless and all caught up in the past.

Ever strive to forgive and align with Love, not so much for the other or because it is the right thing to do, but for yourself.

When we are in revenge or anger or mulling over some old event, the other people are off partying, and we are yet trapped in misery, ruminating over the old event. We apply the Grace of Forgiveness for ourselves so that we can be free to move on and to experience greater good. Forgive and align with Love until you come to the place where literally you do see and you do understand that there was nothing to forgive, in the first place. And that is a mighty High Understanding.

Now, you can move out of needing persons to apologize to you. It is only important to you that you have forgiven them and let the whole thing go. God doesn't need forgiveness. Humans need forgiveness to expand their heart center and to learn to live the Divine Way and to become Love. The human heart and all body parts, since "all is one" are all perfect manifestations of Divine life...God's idea of a perfect system manifest. Remember, the human heart, just like your life, is perfectly sustained on Divine Love, and can go on forever. And this eternal capacity, as in all things that we call physical, represents that inner substance and our great power to daily convert whatever happens to us in our experience. Think about this often ~ how important maintaining the state of Divine Love is to you.

Whatever poisons, angers, or fears come to us, we have the opportunity every day to rise above, to consciously change to Love ~ just like the heart takes that venous blood that is all filled with junk and purifies it and sends it back into the system as pure, wondrous, nurturing blood. So too in daily life, we take into our transcendent hearts experiences, persons, places, things. And we transform the content into purest Love. Before we send our thought, our word out to the universe, we transform that to Love. And, in every instance, you have a choice of how you want to think about something.

You have a choice what you want to project about something. And in this choice is where the great consequence is.

The most important thing to achieve beyond all techniques, beyond all else, the sacred tool that will gain you the Kingdom of utmost Grace, to bless you in all your ways... is the attainment of the Universal Love Consciousness. That is first and foremost, no matter what route you take. It is said, "To him or her who loves much, much is forgiven." And I believe that the Divine Intelligence gives us the experiences and whatever we need to advance further in Highest Love, and we are to perfect those events within ourselves into Love, and return it to the cosmos from whence it came with the purest thought and Blessing of Love, and then we are free.

We have perfected that area, and now can ascend.

When trapped in negative emotion, all that stuff gets into your very cells, cluttering and congesting your physical body. Don't forget ~ your cells are the intelligent life of God. And when you tell yourselves, "I hate that person," or "I won't forgive that person", and you get into it, holding on to all that negative emotion, you are actually streaming poisons into your cells, hurting yourself most of all, not to mention congesting all possibility of renewal for yourself; whereas in consciously cleansing, you open all doors to greater possibility, and enjoy eternally living free of burden in the now.

Thus, the way of cleansing is by consciously striving to be putting Love in, putting God's substance of Love, the thought substance of Love into those cells.

Through steady practice, you want to get to the place where you are moment to moment converting all lower emotion and thought to Love, living completely trace free ~ letting those steel bonds of accumulated karma with that person, place or thing go, replacing all with Love. In this way, dharma and Grace beyond measure is continuously established, lifting you Higher and Higher, with all forces now free in you to establish the Divine Prototypes God has in mind for you.

There is another secret for releasing and dissolving any and all trauma to the physical body. For example, when I fell from the loft, one might describe this as a traumatic event. Although I myself didn't think that, nevertheless it would ordinarily be of concern. Yet, there is a way where any and all trauma to the physical body need not affect us.

Realize that physically and on all levels, no matter what happens to us, it is our resistance to the thing that happens to us that causes the pain.

In one instance, while I had been working on this issue of releasing all trauma of past and present, one of my advanced students who works with some pretty active and volatile, and unpredictable patients, called me to discuss an incident, where one literally had thrown her on a stone floor. And she called me to deal with this, and we talked about this thing of resistance.

As she once again realized that all aspects of her body are light, she was able to let go any thought of permanent damage or harm. Rather than resist, she then simply let the whole event pass through her, allowing the vibration to pass right through her bones, tissues, muscles and all, and as a result, experienced very swift recovery, with no paralysis or injury anywhere. She did not judge it, yet simply went with it, centered in restoring Truth.

The timeless secret of living in the Tao, or going with the flow, is to realize that the body is molecules. It is intelligent molecular form. So if we are relaxed and at ease and go with something, it will just find its way in and through our molecules and out again. It is not that body gets traumatized, yet it is that mind gets traumatized and freezes the condition in space and time ~ fixing the idea within or upon the body. Thus, if I don't heal a thing in my consciousness first, I will not be able to heal, just as when I fell from the loft and I refused to indulge in feelings of fears: "This is severe. This is traumatic. Oh, what a terrible thing." At the very first moment of this critical event that could turn into trauma, I would not fix any negative idea to myself, realizing my idea about it shall become form. Indeed, right there from the yogi position in which I landed, I breathed and began to let the pain pass through.

Instead, I reversed my thoughts and fears by incorporating the *Greater Idea*. I worked on the declaring the exact opposite; "This is nothing. This is nothing to God. Nothing happened here." So if I

234

don't fix a thing in my consciousness, it cannot get stuck in my body. Consciousness goes first. Body follows. Body never makes any determination of its own. Now, we know consciousness animates the body, and consciousness precedes the direction of outcome. Whatever happens in the physical is merely a reflection of the state of consciousness, the idea most deeply held in mind.

In this knowing, I may dissolve any and all conditions, transforming to the perfect Truth at any time, and as regards any trauma, I may simply let it pass through and out the other side. If I don't tighten, resisting with all my might, the body will remain unaffected, just automatically restoring to its normal state of equanimity.

Even if a thing is lodged in me, I may still dissolve it by right thinking. By knowing that it is not a power ~ that consciousness is power. The only thing that needs to be fixed or healed in any situation is our mind. That is the only thing that needs to be transformed. And thus anything that I carry as a traumatic memory in my memory bank, I can now consciously release myself of it, knowing there is no trauma in God.

And it doesn't matter when it was ~ ten years ago, fifteen, thirty, it doesn't matter. Through right knowing now, I can release my body or emotional life from having to hold that trauma that has been given temporary residence there.

Indeed, it is very important for us to go back in time and overview and heal the memories, knowing nothing can attach itself to us ever, unless we give it permission. Know your freedom from the past is a part of the imperishable gifts that come, when realizing you are one with God. Can God be traumatized? There is something that is imperishable about you and that is capable of overcoming all idea of trauma. So by consciously releasing yourself of the impact or whatever negative influence you thought any event may have had on your life, you are freed of it. You can be freed of it right now, regardless of when it happened... Cause, effect and all.

This is a mighty understanding. And all these understandings take practice. It is necessary to practice the consciousness around these things to see your demonstrations...to be able to let go at once that you may renew and prosper in the now. If I have locked a circumstance in my memory, I am the only one who can let it go, by changing my thought about it. For example, right now, let us just each one of us just quickly perform a freeing transformation.

HEALING TRAUMATIC EVENTS

Think of something that you feel has permanently damaged or harmed your Immortal life. Just let your mind think of whatever that is ~ whether it is of a spiritual, emotional, mental or physical nature. Think of a major event that you feel has had a permanent effect on you.

236

Now when you bring that incident and that effect you think it has on you into your mind, replay the circumstance again with a new awareness that you are one with God, with that which is perfect, which cannot be harmed, cannot be diminished, cannot be restricted in any way whatsoever. And decide now to let that memory go, and replace it with an idea of your perfection.

Try to get a realization now and awareness now that "All there is...is God", and the Divine Presence and Power in you is everything that you need to release this memory. *Now see with your inner eye God's light and wisdom and perfect reconstructing action healing up perfectly to perfection whatever area. Take yourself to the point where you realize you never needed to be affected at all. It never happened in God, therefore it never happened in you. It was a nothing to the Divine and Eternal you. Whatever needs to recover, let it recover now. Let go the thought of limitation. Let it drain out of your being completely. Fall away off the body, off your emotions. You are returned to bliss and greatest expectation. You are free.*

These are some of the cleansing tools we always have, and we know that before something new can come to us, we must cleanse our territory, in order to make room for new good because the universe cannot operate in a congested territory. The way to successful overcoming and complete renewal beyond compare is constant cleansing. Cleansing of negative thought and consequent negative emotion is the way that prepares the territory for the Dove

237

of Grace to come upon you, and for the perfect healing needed. Whatever the form of the healing may be, it is all the same to Principle. Cleansing heart and mind prepares a clear space for it to happen. And then, center in Gratitude for the new good you desire.

Your direct tools as a Divine Being for healing your body, your circumstances, and everything you do are always with you, as you...Divine Light and Breath. You may direct the inner light of Divine Intelligence to any area of the body that you would like to see healed, and see the issue corrected, visualizing the Light performing all transformational healing that need to be. Breath is life and breath is God. You can breathe that Prana, that invisible breath between every breath, the real breath of God that the ancient yogis live on... and just as those Masters who live on Divine Prana find the bliss beyond comprehension, you too will be filled with the rich and radiant substance of ever-renewing life at hand.

Through taking time to breathe the elixir of the Divine Breath into a certain area and shining the light of your consciousness, loaded with the nurturing substance of Divine Spirit, you can perfect any and all healings.

And you can perform any cleansing necessary that way, whether it be for heart, lung, muscle, bone, or tissue. See the regenerating Light of God there, doing the perfect work. Meditate often on your system, on clearing it out, declaring and Giving

Thanks that everything is in perfect Divine Order, everything is expressing the perfect Balance, Harmony, Order, and Radiance of God. Start regularly using the direct healing tools you have. If you are going to doctors of any sort, help them help you by contemplating yourself in the healed condition desired.

Help the doctors help you by doing the right thing in consciousness, knowing only the Presence of Divine Truth, Capacity, and Light at work in your condition, no matter what appears. If you really do this in full, eventually you will build up such dynamic energy and power in your capacity to focus the all-encompassing Light that you will be able to heal at once. Breathe deeply, when meditating on the Light. Your breath is the source of your life. And breath is all power of renewal. And what are those Yogis, Saints and Masters doing, but building up that vital energy through and through, that radiant substance that is the very force of life ~ to be able to direct it wherever, to handle whatever may come. You have Breath, and you have Light, and you have Love and Faith beyond all measure. And I believe if you combine all those, you have got the quintessential elements of the great alchemists.

Remember, the use of your will is the other significant factor, your power to choose the path you will walk. Will expresses most perfectly when aligned with the perfect will of life, another word for God…another word for love, for perfection, for joy, for abundance, for harmony…the many, many names of the Sublime.

Will accomplishes in complete and most exalted efficacy when aligned with the essence of the Divine Nature. Herein, there is no discord, as you sound the symphony of the One, the great Aum of the Universe. And, when you apply and use your will to determine to manifest all that is good, true, beautiful, and worthy of a Divine Being ~ you are using it at the Highest Level with no harm to anyone. Some people call this surrendering to the will of God. I call it joining the will of God, conscious joining the will of life itself.

And, knowing that the will of life is to perpetuate that which it is, we ever want to use all our God-given faculties of Light, Love, Wisdom, centered in the Holy Breath …intelligently and with the power of will directed towards this noble purpose of demonstrating the completeness and all-capacity of the Divine Life Force.

Realize that subconsciously, we are always make pathways to our future in our very own mind by the substance of the majority of beliefs. Decisions about the destiny of our individual life are commensurate or equal to that. And, it is so important to become aware of the inner decisions you have made, for these determinations, known or unknown, become a projection that goes before you. Always Spirit, the inner substance of the idea being held in mind, goes before, on invisible planes drawing the equivalent experience on outer levels. Our inner vision precedes every single manifestation that you and I will have. And in order to transcend all notions connected with death and dying, one needs to heal every thought and belief contrary to the Immortal Principles and ever-renewing life of God within. Death is the culmination of all negative ideas. The chief repository of any and all negativity has accumulated to become this thing called death. Death is the condition humans have created as the big supermarket for all negatives.

Yet, remember ~ "Wherever I go, there I am, so live life every moment to the fullest right now, achieving and implementing as much Higher Awareness that you can. If you do so, your life will be incrementally better and better no matter what plane of existence you are on.

Thus, in order to change, to really make a powerful change in the course of destiny, we must make an inner change with whatever we have decided about that moment of transition from the earthy plane.

Do you believe that God is the author of Life, in which no death and only eternal transformation, resurrection and ascension exists?

This is the exalted power of the Divine Will of life in us, where we ourselves are free to make any decision we choose, and to experience the consequences of our choices. We understand we are in charge. All Divine Authority is ours. In the province of will, we can choose however long we want to live. There is no force that is saying you have to go at this time or that time. It is totally up to us to choose the entire period of time that we choose to be in this body and to utilize this form in Highest and Best ways, for we shall always have a form, whether as a beautiful human or a beam of light.

Know that so long as this form serves your good purposes, you are entitled to live in it as the most wonderful vehicle of transportation ~ your body home, your gorgeous apartment, as it were, with a never-ending lease. Whenever you sign a lease, one of the codicils states that it is your right to live in the home in peace, joy and happiness. Never forget that you are the one who decides however long, not some force of fate.

We want to direct all our efforts towards living the exalted Will of Eternal Life, living our Immortality in the Now, utilizing the great gifts of eternal maintenance and expansion that we have been so graciously endowed with, extending our life giving properties as far as we can.

Let us close now in deepest Gratitude, knowing that each is establishing the Path of Divine Grace and transcendence of every issue that needs. And what I would like to do is just to be able to assist you to create a new relationship with this idea.

Now, let us take a moment to raise ourselves up to new and heightened levels, never before considered. The following is a meditation, where you can experience the most lustrous, Infinite, possible future for yourself…Just a wonderful experience that I'd like you to have.

EXTENDING YOUR LIFE INDEFINITELY

Changing Your Destiny

Once again, let us go within, letting all thoughts of this moment drop away…just letting all concern of any sort leave our being and bringing our consciousness into the great causal center of being, realizing that we are setting a new cause for our lives, each one according to his or her greatest vision.

And, Once again, let us take a deep, vitalizing breath, breathing in and out of the Immortal breath, the breath of God, of Life itself, all Truth, all sublime knowing…rising up through every chakra. As you breathe deeply, in and out of the radiance of Divine Life, gently rise now into your Higher-Mind, up through the top of your head, stepping out of the body shell, now standing free in the vast universal substance of Light and Love…one with God, with Infinite Good and Love and Light.

One now, at the summit of all existence, one with First Cause…realize you can change anything that is not of your Divine Pattern. Anything the Father hath not established has come to pass by virtue of the Divine You!

243

Grateful for the true freedom you have, take a look from your High Place now, a moment to overview your whole life stream, in particular turning your mind to view all the current attitudes and opinions in your thought field, those thoughts and feelings that have been governing your life up until now. And now I'd like you to view the force and the magnetic field of all those persons around you.

In your vast overview, include even your own memories and all, and just get a real overview.

Now, once you have found and defined this current point in your timeline for yourself and you can see it all very clearly, I'd like you to move in consciousness, leaving this scenario and moving into the future to the point where you think, feel or believe that you have established a point of expectancy of physical death or the start of deterioration on any level for yourself.

Moving slowly through time, observing the years, the decades, see if you can locate where it is.

Now, looking at that point that you had established in your mind before, envision it and consider it. Think about or consider if you would like to place a new option there, if you'd like to change your decree about yourself and perhaps you would even like to commune with your High Self to discuss the possibility of something greater?

Consider that you may change your decision, change your decree to see now a new and greater option than ever before. What is that new option that lays before you, that is so thrilling and magnificent?

In the moment, envision your radiant Higher Self, the one that sits at the right hand of the Father, the blessed one that knows no division between itself and God ~ The perfect Light Body. Have a conversation with your Higher Self, which is radiating its complete beneficence and wisdom towards you now. Ask your Divine Self what you want to know.

When the answer comes, thank your Infinite Self, your Cosmic Self, one with God, your perfect self for always being there for you, and for revealing the far Greater Option that you have.

Once you have considered this new option, view yourself passing over this point, this former point with ease... safe and secure with your entire body physical intact.

See yourself passing through the same point with ease and complete success, with your mind on your new option. You have arrived safe and sound, rejoicing, filled with the breath and life of God, radiant in all your ways, renewed, joyous and vital... Happy you have chosen to take your Divine Body with you and that you have chosen to maintain it aright and to know a new thing.

See yourself filled with the radiance of Divine Victory. The breath of God fills your every cell. See yourself so happy to be living such a wonderful life, so in awe to be free of that former limitation, so thrilled that you have broken that chain of negative cause/effect and established yourself anew.

Now, think back to what was it? What was it that prompted you to change? What was it that prompted you to extend your life for yourself? What new idea came to you through your Higher Self that knows your possibilities completely? What new options and visions do you now have that you hold very dear? For, remember, without vision the people perish. What is your vision? What does God, your Highest mind, your High Self of Love and Infinite Good, what greatness does your Infinite Self have in mind for you now?

Now, take this new option, this gift and pearl, this priceless treasure that you have been given, and extend your vision now as far as you want, realizing it is your choice to go as far as you want in the glorious stream of life expressing through you. Know you are no poised to go so much further than you had ever imagined.

Immersing yourself in the wonder of it all, thank your Higher Self whose level you are on right now... for all of the great information and the glorious vision it has given to you. Thank your beautiful Higher Self that has extended your vision further for as far as you want, seeing your life expressing anew.

246

And, when you are ready, say goodbye to your Higher Self with whom you are always one and give heartfelt Thanks, remembering the new course of fruitful living now available to you. Thank it for assisting you and when you are ready, remember your new decision, and return to the present in your own time.

Persons always have such marvelous and transcendent experiences, while taking time to contemplate a far greater future.

One gymnast, found her body felt entirely renewed. "It was wonderful. I saw myself tumbling in absolute joy!"

"You know, I love gymnastics!"

She had unconsciously figured that when she got older, she wouldn't have a lot of energy. That had probably been a sore spot all her life, a point of deep sadness that she was harboring within… this limited view of herself, this limited view of her future, and she never even knew it. Now her spirit was freed to soar, and her new option to maintain endless flexibility had released so much of her original enthusiasm, vigor, buoyancy and vitality back to her.

Another found herself healing all of her money issues at once, as she contemplated Infinite Divine Substance of Supply … "Transforming all of my moneys to contain more zeros". No more would she have to live in any form of old limitation.

In her mind's eye, she became a superb manifestor, learning the art of materializing Divine and unlimited substance as money. The prospect alone of always being free to create more made more life worth hanging out for. There now would be no more limit as to how much good she could create, as she relied upon Principle and kept her consciousness on Unlimited Supply. "It pays off."

Another saw himself around people involved in pursuit of Highest Spiritual Understanding, and adding to the Spiritual Awareness of society…A teacher, or somebody doing spiritual work, going out to spots where spiritual work is done, a form of work and service that he would love so much so that there would be no feeling of working at all. He was really enjoying himself, no longer feeling oppressed like before.

And so it is that no matter how far one has progressed, one doesn't stop doing, serving and contributing. Yet, our efforts become more refined, and more perfectly harmonious with our true natures,' and as we proceed to open up to greater life-giving possibilities without end, the images for rewarding self-expression pour forth. The ways and means of accomplishment are ever the same ~ keeping our minds on High, living transcendent and centered in Truth, knowing only the Divine Presence and Power at all times at the helm of our lives, doing all we can to transform emotions, and to walk the talk in our everyday life, having that Faith against which no negative can stand.

Realize, we can go on these inner journeys at any time, by meditating within, and should often... envisioning the brightest possible future for ourselves, because like Christ said it is not enough to eliminate something or say no, we have got to now extend our vision beyond the parameters and boundaries we perceived ourselves in before... to get a greater vision for ourselves because truly without vision the people perish.

Every time, we have a vision that is greater than our now state, that gives the length of our will a place to go to, to form. But if you say it is over at a certain point, that is it.

Constantly evolve your inner pictures of yourself to greater and more fulfilling stages. Stretch your consciousness to include the good, the better, and the best every moment. Feel your possibilities in God, and place your whole confidence in an eternally wonderful future for yourself. Feed it with your good vision and practice expanding your vision for yourself always to include the greatest concepts that speak of life unfolding on greater and greater, more richly rewarding planes of existence. Always be extending your vision to include greater, greater, greater, greater.

So you see, the whole thing of destiny all rests in our choice. The future is our decision, and our vision precedes us... Vision and decision lead the way. Daily determine the Highest and Best Outcomes for yourself, filled with the radiance of the Divine.

If you can realize how powerful your consciousness is, you will guard your thought patterns. And as many great ones have said, strive to get to the place where nothing proceeds from your consciousness save that you which you would like to see manifest in your life return to you.

There was a time, and many times I am sure, when cultures have come to the glorious point we are at now, where they have become transcendent, have opened up to the secrets, have learned their identity, and then somehow got caught in power-plays, and the collective society failed to grab hold and rise one rung further. Yet, there was a time when not one negative thought was entertained. If you looked up in Webster's Dictionary "the beginning of time," you wouldn't see one negative word. Persons wouldn't even have known what that was.

So it is for the individual to stream out all of this accumulated negativity, remembering negativity equals death, and to the degree that we are hanging out in a negative thought field, we are careening toward that unfortunate fate...encumbering and limiting the beautiful Immortal Light within, ladening ourselves with more burden, and moving right toward an unwanted destiny ~ just playing the old scenario out all over again.

The only way straight up and out is by practicing right thought, right action, right knowing of who you are in essence...the

Immortal life of the Creator Divine. Never forget. It doesn't matter what the feeling is or what may be going on in your life, you always want to remain centered in Divine Awareness of your beloved Divine and Immortal Self. This is called "living beyond appearances", and the guarantee of certain outstanding success, knowing; "Regardless of whatever appears, I am one with God." This force is the mighty force that causes you to walk on the water, to soar above and beyond the vicissitudes of the world, victorious in every challenge.

This is the force that is transcendent and whereby you can change literally your magnetic field to become a radiant field of Light. It is very easy to succumb to the lesser, and the human aspect just wants to get into those feelings, to get into the stuff. Yet, all of that just drags us down, binding us to the wheel of repetition and creating more bondage. It is only by conscious choice that we can stop ourselves midstream and change the trajectory of destiny, by using the Divine capacity of self-observation, exercising our gift of choice and consciously changing so that only that which we want to experience as our living reality proceeds from our every sacred silent thought, expectation and action.

Place no caps on yourself ~ knowing the completeness of the Divine is in you. Think not in terms of time and space ~ only in terms of manifesting greater and greater Light in the Eternal Now ~ the spark becoming the Immortal Flame.

251

See yourself as you would like to be. Get the consciousness that each stage is only the beginning ~ as you rise Higher and Higher into the beneficence of your Heavenly Estate. There is no limit as to how much you can accomplish, to how far you may go, as you relate ever more closely to the Divine-in-You.

Realize all around you... from relationships to career are opportunities to establish that firm foundation of Love, and to cultivate Divine attributes to stand by you all of your Immortal life.

You are Forever, and all else has come to pass. Put the gold dust of your blessing Infinite nature in all you do, embracing all in your Cosmic Heart ~ yet never attaching to any in your Immortal stream, establishing Dharma everywhere you go. Each is God calling to you to bring that Love that surpasseth all understanding.

Learn to regenerate every moment, realizing the Eternally Resurrecting One is in you.

Make yourself a place for Divine Grace to appear, by being Love and Highest Expectations in all things ~ both near and far, both small and everyday, and just as large and quantum as can be.

Know Divine Love is with you morning, noon and night ~ every moment flowing in Grace to you, over, around, in and through. Within its orb, there is nothing you cannot do.

~

And I know that the Divine Power and Intelligence has been abiding over us and working through each one of us to bring exactly the information each one needs, the understanding to move into greater levels of expression. I know that it is accomplished, and I know that each one goes forth a radiance of Truth, demonstrating, manifesting and projecting that sublime Truth through their life to all other lives on this planet. We are choosing Immortality.

Choose Immortality. So what if it takes a while to get there? At least we are choosing. And now the door is open to unlimited experience of well-being, heretofore unknown.

May all Infinite Blessings be yours without ceasing!
Aum! Bliss!

And So It Is!

Testimonial/Review by Richard Harvey
Author/ "Your Sacred Calling!"

The author, Reverend Dr. Linda De Coff, of this transcendent book, Immortality Now and Forever, is eminently placed to impart knowledge of the Divine realms and their relationship to our human experience of flux and change. She states the case that in this present moment Heaven is on Earth and through her clear and passionate prose, laced with transcendental exercises, inspiring stories, affirmations, meditations, and prayers, she speaks to us of the Timeless Truth that God, the Divine, is truly ubiquitous and inevitable. Our Higher Mind, she points out compellingly, *is* the Divine Nature. Death is a fallacy, a product of delusion and we are free to live our lives in self-renewal, perpetual change and creativity, and radiate Divine Light.

~

De Coff's emphasis on steady practice is sound and timely and practical as she offers an abundance of exercises for the aspirant and reveals the secrets of the spiritual path as one can only do who offers authentic wisdom and illumination. Her knowing is surely from her own direct experience as she exemplifies over and over again. Accessing that which is beyond mind, indescribable and unsayable, she teaches how to negotiate your way through the seduction of emotional states and heal past trauma.

~

What she states is surely incontrovertibly right: when we are One with God all is well. An impassioned guide firmly located in the locus of truth, De Coff guides the reader out of fear and confusion to a vision of a marvelous destiny, as she exhorts us to: "Try to realize that every one of us comprises the one body ~ God's body, the Divine Manifestation… A Universal Body Perfect of the One Perfect One."

NEW THOUGHT INTERNATIONAL

(An Association of Global Centers for World Peace & Enlightenment)

Dear Reader ~ It is our pleasure to announce that downloads of Dr. Linda's books and talks are now available for purchase, directly from our library at NEW THOUGHT INTERNATIONAL, INC.

New Thought International Library Special Catalog

If you wish to arrange to formally receive Spiritual Mind Treatment, please advise Dr. Linda of your interest at **REVDECOFF@AOL.COM.**

All are welcome, whether new to the Science of Mind or highly trained. The possibilities of healing any matter are blissfully infinite in scope, so each can gain immeasurably.

I highly recommend my book, **SONGS OF ETERNITY (PART I ~ THE PRINCIPLE, Declarations of the Immortal Soul of God) and (PART II ~ THE APPLICATION,** *Bringing Heaven To Earth* **!)** containing the Manifesting Key and Universal Self-Existent Principle for every situation from Divine Fulfillment to Divine Creation to Divine Prosperity, Healing, Immortality and Romance.

Each short Instruction is followed by an empowering "I Am" Meditation for incorporating deep within.

I am so pleased to say that SONGS OF ETERNITY ~ Contemplations, Treatments and Meditations on the Word of God **is now available in all e*book formats exclusively on Amazon.com. These convenient formats allow easy instant navigation to any subject you desire to focus and meditate on. Paperback is also available on all familiar sites.**

To Purchase and for free preview: Visit:

http://www.amazon.com/Linda-De-Coff/e/B006J351EM/ref=dp_byline_cont_book_1

GLOBAL DIVINE CONSCIOUSNESS SERIES

OTHER PUBLISHED BOOKS INCLUDE:

BRIDGE OF THE GODS, A Handbook for Ascending Humanity~ *The Golden Pathway to your Highest God Self!*

SONGS OF ETERNITY~ *Contemplations, Treatments and Meditations on the Word of God!*

DIVINE ROMANCE & PERFECT PARTNERSHIP~ *The Immortal Principles & Powers of Divine Love!*

LIVING THE MIRACLE CONSCIOUSNESS, *Attaining The Kingdom of Greatest Eternal Good ~ Heaven on Earth!*

THE LEGACY OF THE COSMIC CHRIST ~ *The Return of the Cosmic Christ!*

MYSTICISM & ULTIMATE DIVINE HEALING PROCESSES ~ THE PERFECT PRINCIPLES AND PATTERNS OF GOD!

DIVINE PROSPERITY ~ *The Unexpected Income Program, "12 Steps To Your Perfect Consciousness of Infinite and Eternal Supply"*

~

In all the books, comprising her *Global Divine Consciousness Series*, *Dr. Linda De Coff* touches every condition of life with astonishing clarity and luminosity, providing enlightening keys for the reader on how to raise yourself every day in every way to become the *Divine Plan* fulfilled.

TO PLACE YOUR ORDERS ~ VISIT

HTTP://NEWTHOUGHTINTERNATIONAL.COM/
BOOKSANDTAPES.HTML

*Visit and preview Dr. Linda's Author Page and currently available books on Amazon.: **http://www.amazon.com/Linda-De-Coff/e/B006J351EM/ref=dp_byline_cont_book_1**

BRIDGE OF THE GODS ~ The Golden Pathway to Your Highest God Self!; SONGS OF ETERNITY ~ Contemplations, Treatments and Meditations on the Word of God; LIVING THE MIRACLE CONSCIOUSNESS ~ Attaining the Kingdom of Greatest Eternal Good!"

 Join Dr. Linda on her Pages:

http://www.authorsden.com/visit/viewwork.asp?id=59977

Visit & Follow Dr. Linda on Facebook ~ on Linked In

Visit Dr. Linda's You Tube Channel ~ for full length Talks & Meditations on Higher Consciousness Themes.

Visit Dr. Linda's Blog and Archives for Current Free Monthly Articles & Programs on "Attaining Divine Consciousness"

Dr. Linda is also on Linked In. All are welcome to join her group, "The Next Step in Spiritual Advancement"

Visit and Follow Dr. Linda on Twitter and Keep Up To Date on Special Events, Book Giveaways and More.

FORMULA FOR SPIRITUAL MIND TREATMENT ~ For Your convenience!

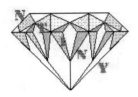

1. Recognition ~ I recognize there is a Principle of Perfect _____(fill in with the words most describing the Infinite Resource that you want to participate in and that is your "Solution"), i.e. if in lack of any sort, affirm the "Principle of Perfect Supply".

2. Unification ~ I, (the true I Am and God Self within every being) am one with that! Now, you are moving away from empowering the problem to empowering your Highest God-Self within and all surrounding, the one and only solution to every issue.

3. Realization ~ Because I recognize **I am one with all the great Divine Principles of the Universe,** I now declare the glad Truth about my situation_____. Let your realization include all the elements necessary as you think of your life as One with God, i.e. no time, no space, no difficulty, no limit. Let your Realization rise to the level of knowing your Good is available right now. Remember, you are not relying upon yourself or any limited history you may have (as apart from the Divine) ~ yet you are now radically and directly relying upon the Greatest Power that is, God and Universal Mind and Substance within. Realize you can choose to live in the penthouse of your thoughts, or in the basement. Always choose to rise to the Highest level, always available to you.

4. Thanksgiving ~ I give thanks! Let your heart overflow with Gratitude to God, Infinite Substance and Supply for all you have and the more to come. Describe in most radiant detail.

5. Release ~ I release! When you are ready and feel you have reached the maximum depths of awareness in your treatment.........

Then take a deep breath of God and declare your release in Faith to the Great Wisdom and Power that is bringing all about in perfection beyond imagining.

GLOBAL DIVINE CONSCIOUSNESS SERIES

It has been said of Dr. Linda's glowing works ~

"You cannot be the same on the other side of these reads!" ~ *Michael Ben Zehabe, Author, Syndicated Columnist*

"Just reading one chapter can lift your consciousness for an entire day!" ~ *Deborah Beauvais, Owner Dreamvisions7 Radio Network via NBC Radio Boston*

"I was captivated from page one!" ~ *Barry Finlay, Award winning author/Kilimanjaro & Beyond!*

"An amazing addition to the World's greatest Spiritual and Philosophical Books...Worth its weight in gold!" ~ *Jeanne Latter, Actress/ Screenwriter/Director"*

"Dr. Linda helped me remember my magnificence." ~ *Claire Louise Roberts/Attorney*

"One wonderful thing after another has happened and only 3 days after starting the Unexpected Income Program"! ~ *Mel Thompson, Teacher*

"This is a book to be read not once or twice... but to have near you to reflect Divine grace from and into you, to realize your Oneness with All in Consciousness." ~ *Testimonial Review/ Richard Harvey/Author/Your Sacred Calling!*

MYSTICISM & DIVINE HEALING

Discover the Profound Healing Secrets of the Mystics of the Ages, and learn how to Identify with the Limitless Divine Principles and Capacity of God-within-you.

~

Live the Life of Miraculous Healing in every Department of concern.

Understand the Divine Principles always available to you, and the way to activate through applying the Highest Consciousness of Spiritual Mind Treatment ~ Your Ultimate Healing Tool!

261

LIVING YOUR IMMORTALITY NOW!

~

HOW TO LIVE FOREVER ~
IN YOUR DIVINE BODY OF LIGHT! ~

*

PUBLISHED BY REVEREND DR. LINDA DECOFF

AND

NEW THOUGHT INTERNATIONAL, INC.

*

VISIT OUR WEBSITE AT:

HTTP://NEWTHOUGHTINTERNATIONAL.COM

*

VISIT DR. LINDA'S WEBSITE

HTTP://REVDRLINDADECOFF.COM